'Words for Christmas'

By Candlelight

Selected for *'Caprice'* by Jon Vaughan
Illustrated by Ken Rolf

An anthology of Christmas Readings
as selected for the Candlelit Supper Concerts of
Caprice - The Essex Wind Orchestra

Sold in aid of:

Farleigh Hospice, Essex Air Ambulance, The Home Farm Trust
*60% of all profits from the sale of this book will be distributed between these
charities. The remainder will be allocated by Caprice through its fundraising for the
various other Charities supported by its friends and members.
A full list of charities supported and monies raised can be found at:-*
www.capricewindorchestra.org.uk

Dedication

To Joy Bome and all the various members of *'Caprice'*, past and present, who continue to provide so much pleasure and entertainment for so many in Essex and beyond, through their concerts and recordings and especially in helping to make Christmas special and so much fun each year.

Introduction

Christmas has always meant something very special to me. Besides the wonderful and often magical qualities of the traditional story with its simplicity and humble setting, there have been so many interesting customs associated with this time of the year, in nearly every country in the world.

Having grown up in a family with a German Mother, from an early age I can remember the excitement which started with the visits of Father Christmas on each Saturday night in Advent, to fill our slippers which had been left on the stairs in ready anticipation of the gifts of marzipan, 'Lebkuchen' biscuits, chocolate Christmas figures, nuts and tangerines. The smell on discovery on Advent Sunday mornings was intoxicating. We always enjoyed a candlelight tea on each Sunday, again with delicacies from Germany, (having relatives there was a big advantage for Mr Claus!) and following the traditional get together, often with visitors and friends, we all crowded into the sitting room and listened to my Father reading each successive stave of Dickens' 'A Christmas Carol'. I feel sure that it is from this yearly activity that I learned to appreciate good literature, a love for the books of Dickens and how to read aloud with an attentive audience in mind. I haven't got the space to recount the actual celebrations at Christmastide but suffice it to say, these too were some of the most magical memories of my childhood with candles on the tree on Christmas Eve followed by present opening, followed by a traditional High Tea and much excitement. All this had been preceded by a walk during the afternoon and listening to the Nine Lessons and Carols from King's College Chapel in Cambridge.

Whilst teaching Drama at KEGS in Chelmsford I had the good fortune to meet Joy who was assisting with the music as a Peripatetic teacher. As an evening class at another local school, she had recently set up a small wind orchestra which was gradually swelling in numbers. Following extensive rehearsals, these musicians were now ready to play in public. From there started the Candlelight suppers and my connection with Caprice as a reader for the occasion. Throughout the years that have followed I have had enormous pleasure in selecting suitable extracts to fill in with the more traditional first part of the programme and a lighter and

CAPRICE - THE ESSEX WIND ORCHESTRA

How many people have had the opportunity to do what they love doing and finish up with a book dedicated to them? Jon has done so many beautiful readings at our Candlelit Concerts, sometimes serious, sometimes sad, sometimes in dialects and sometimes so funny that they have caused great laughter. The opportunity to be able to have a book of them to read for ourselves is very exciting. We have had so many wonderful times over many years and to be able to turn back the clock and relive some of those moments is a great privilege.

Caprice the Essex Wind Orchestra was formed in 1987 as a small group of 11 players within the adult education system. We began, and continue, to rehearse once a week during school term at Boswells School in Springfield, Chelmsford, Essex. We have now grown to a large orchestra of 80 players. Some people live many miles away and others locally.

One of the things which became apparent after a few weeks was the need to give a concert to show the results of our labours. After a 'try out' concert for families and friends we booked our first concert and decided to give the profits to charity. The music and the giving have grown hugely, and to date we have helped to raise £105,000 and the work continues. We have great support from families and Patrons as well as other donations for which we are so grateful and without which we would be unable to continue to work in this way.

We believe that to be able to meet for rehearsals, give concerts for

Contents

A Humorous Christmas

The True Meaning of Christmas

Closing Sentiments

Acknowledgements   97

A CHRISTMAS SALUTATION
Fra Giovanni

I salute you! There is nothing I can give you which you have not; but there is much, that, while I cannot give, you can take.

No Heaven can come to us unless our hearts find rest in it today.
Take Heaven.

No peace lies in the future which is not hidden in this present instant.
Take Peace.

The gloom of the world is but a shadow; behind it, yet, within our reach, is joy.
Take Joy.

And so, at this Christmas time, I greet you with the prayer that for you, now and for-ever, the day breaks and the shadows flee away.

A Nostalgic Christmas

CAROLS IN GLOUCESTERSHIRE
from 'Cider With Rosie' by Laurie Lee

Later, towards Christmas, there was heavy snow, which raised the roads to the top of the hedges. There were millions of tons of the lovely stuff, plastic, pure, all-purpose, which nobody owned, which one could carve or tunnel, eat, or just throw about. It covered the hills and cut off the villages, but nobody thought of rescues; for there was hay in the barns and flour in the kitchens, the women baked bread, the cattle were fed and sheltered-we'd been cut off before, after all.

The week before Christmas, when snow seemed to lie thickest, was the moment for carol-singing, and when I think back to those nights it is to the crunch of snow and to the lights of the lanterns on it. Carol-singing in my village was a special tithe for the boys, the girls had little to do with it. Like hay-making, black-berrying, stone-clearing and wishing-people-a-happy-Easter, it was one of our seasonal perks.

By instinct we knew just when to begin it; a day too soon and we should have been unwelcome, a day too late and we should have received lean looks from people whose bounty was already exhausted. When the true moment came, exactly balanced, we recognized it and were ready.

A maid bore the tidings of our arrival away into the echoing distances of the house, and while we waited we cleared our throats noisily. Then she came back, and the door was left ajar for us, and we were bidden to begin. We brought no music, the carols were in our heads. "Let's give 'em 'Wild Shepherds', " said Jack. We began in confusion, plunging into a wreckage of keys, of different words and tempo; but we gathered our strength; he who sang loudest took the rest of us with him, and the carol took shape if not sweetness.

This huge stone house, with its ivied walls, was always a mystery to us. What were those gables, those rooms and attics, those narrow windows veiled by the cedar trees? As we sang 'Wild Shepherds' we craned our necks, gaping into that lamp-lit hall which we had never entered; staring at the muskets and untenanted chairs, the great tapestries furred by dust - until suddenly, on the stairs, we saw the old Squire himself standing and listening with his head on one side.

He didn't move until we'd finished; then slowly he tottered towards us, dropped two coins in our box with a trembling hand, scratched his name in the book we carried, gave us each a long look with his moist blind eyes, then turned away in silence.

As though released from a spell, we took a few sedate steps, then broke into a run for the gate. We didn't stop till we were out of the grounds. Impatient, at last, to discover the extent of his bounty, we squatted by the cowsheds, held our lanterns over the book, and saw that he had written 'Two Shillings'. This was quite a good start. No one of any worth in the district would dare to give us less than the Squire.

So with money in the box, we pushed on up the valley, pouring scorn on each other's performance. Confident now, we began to consider our quality and whether one carol was not better suited to us than another. Horace, Walt said, shouldn't sing at all; his voice was beginning to break. Horace disputed this and there was a brief token battle - they fought as they walked, kicking up divots of snow, then they forgot it, and Horace still sang.

Steadily we worked through the length of the valley, going from house to house, visiting the lesser and the greater gentry - the farmers, the doctors, the merchants, the majors and other exalted persons. It was freezing hard and blowing too; yet not for a moment did we feel the cold.

this. As always it was late; as always this was our final call. The snow had a fine crust upon it, and the old trees sparkled like tinsel.

We grouped ourselves round the farmhouse porch. The sky cleared, and broad streams of stars ran down over the valley and away to Wales. On Slad's white slopes, seen through the black sticks of its woods, some red lamps still burned in the windows.

Everything was quiet; everywhere there was the faint crackling silence of the winter night. We started singing, and we were all moved by the words and the sudden trueness of our voices. Pure, very clear, and breathless we sang:

> As Joseph was a-walking
> He heard an angel sing;
> "This night shall be the birth-time
> Of Christ the Heavenly King.
> He neither shall be bornèd
> In Housen nor in hall,
> Nor in a place of paradise
> But in an ox's stall. . . ."

And 2,000 Christmases became real to us then; the houses, the halls, the places of paradise had all been visited; the stars were bright to guide the Kings through the snow; and across the farmyard we could hear the beasts in their stalls. We were given roast apples and hot mince-pies, in our nostrils were spices like myrrh, and in our wooden box, as we headed back for the village, there were golden gifts for all.

A CHILD'S CHRISTMAS IN WALES
by Dylan Thomas

One Christmas was so much like another, in those years around the sea-town corner now and out of all sound except the distant speaking of the voices I sometimes hear a moment before sleep, that I can never remember whether it snowed for six days and six nights when I was twelve or whether it snowed for twelve days and twelve nights when I was six.

All the Christmases roll down toward the two-tongued sea, like a

Prothero standing in the middle of them, waving his slipper as though he were conducting.

"Do something," he said.

And we threw all our snowballs into the smoke - I think we missed Mr Prothero - and ran out of the house to the telephone box.

"Let's call the police as well," Jim said.

"And the ambulance."

"And Ernie Jenkins, he likes fires."

But we only called the fire brigade, and soon the fire engine came and three tall men in helmets brought a hose into the house and Mr Prothero got out just in time before they turned it on. Nobody could have had a noisier Christmas Eve. And when the firemen turned off the hose and were standing in the wet, smoky room, Jim's aunt, Miss Prothero, came downstairs and peered in at them. Jim and I waited, very quietly, to hear what she would say to them. She said the right thing, always. She looked at the three tall firemen in their shining helmets, standing among the smoke and cinders and dissolving snowballs, and she said:
"Would you like anything to read?"

CHRISTMAS IS COMING
from 'The Country Child' by Alison Uttley

At Christmas the wind ceased to moan. Snow lay thick on the fields and the woods cast blue shadows across it. The fir trees were like sparkling, gem-laden Christmas trees, the only ones Susan had ever seen. The orchard, with the lacy old boughs outlined with snow, was a grove of fairy trees. The woods were enchanted, exquisite, the trees were holy, and anything harmful had shrunken to a thin wisp and had retreated into the depths.

The fields lay with their unevennesses gone and paths obliterated, smooth white slopes criss-crossed by black lines running up to the woods.

The floor of the apple chamber was covered with apples, rosy apples, little yellow ones like cowslip balls, wizenedy apples with withered, wrinkled cheeks, fat, well-fed smooth-faced apples, and immense green cookers, pointed like a house, which would burst in the oven and pour out a thick cream of the very essence of apples.

Even the cheese chamber had its cheeses this year, for there had been too much milk for the milkman, and the cheese presses had been put into use again. Some of them were Christmas cheese, with layers of sage running through the middles like green ribbons.

Stone jars like those in which the forty thieves hid stood on the pantry floor, filled with white lard, and balls of fat tied up in bladders hung from the hooks. Along the broad shelves round the walls were pots of jam, blackberry and apple from the woods and orchard, Victoria plum from the trees on house and barn, black currant from the garden, and red currant jelly, damson cheese from the half-wild ancient trees which grew everywhere, leaning over walls, dropping their blue fruit on paths and walls, in pigsty and orchard, in field and water trough, so that Susan thought they were wild as hips and haws.

Pickles and spices filled old brown pots decorated with crosses and flowers, like the pitchers and crocks of Will Shakespeare's time.

In the little dark wine chamber under the stairs were bottles of elderberry wine, purple, thick, and sweet, and golden cowslip wine, and hot ginger, some of them many years old, waiting for the winter festivities.

There were dishes piled with mince pies on the shelves of the larder, and a row of plum puddings with their white calico caps, and strings of sausages, and round pats of butter, with swans and cows and wheat-ears printed upon them.

Everyone who called at the farm had to eat and drink at Christmas-tide.

A few days before Christmas Mr. Garland and Dan took a bill-hook and knife and went into the woods to cut branches of scarlet-berried holly. They tied them together with ropes and dragged them down over the fields to the barn. Mr. Garland cut a bough of mistletoe from the ancient hollow hawthorn which leaned over the wall by the orchard, and thick clumps of dark-berried ivy from the walls.

Indoors, Mrs. Garland and Susan and Becky polished and rubbed

Twisted candles hung down, yellow, red, and blue, unlighted but gay, and on either side was a string of paper lanterns.

Mrs. Garland climbed on a stool and nailed on the wall the Christmas texts, 'God bless our Home', 'God is Love', 'Peace be on this House', 'A Happy Christmas and a Bright New Year'.

So the preparations were made. Susan hung up her stocking at the foot of the bed and fell asleep. But soon singing roused her and she sat, bewildered. Yes, it was the carol-singers.

Outside under the stars she could see the group of men and women, with lanterns throwing beams across the paths and on to the stable door. One man stood apart beating time, another played a fiddle and another had a flute. The rest sang in four parts the Christmas hymns, 'While shepherds watched', 'O come, all ye faithful', and 'Hark the herald angels sing'.

There was the Star; Susan could see it twinkling and bright in the dark boughs with their white frosted layers; and there was the stable. In a few hours it would be Christmas Day, the best day of all the year.

PEACE ON EARTH
by Nina Mansell

Nina Mansell, a fellow of the Institute of Journalists, has contributed this account of her first family Christmas as a wife and mother with a new baby, in war-torn south-east London.

It must be a family Christmas. On this I was determined, now that I had my small son in my arms. My husband would be unlikely to be called out on bomb disposal duty, and my mother was so frail that such an opportunity could not be postponed until another year. It would be my small testament to the unity of the family: three generations sharing a well-needed festivity.

But if we were to be together, it needed long-term planning for although actual fighting had ceased, the ghost of war had not been laid to rest. Our eyes had grown accustomed to ruins, to make-do-and-mend, to cold and damp homes with their inadequate heating and draughty windows

few oranges, chestnuts, uncooked beetroot, sausages, Coalite, wooden boxes for kindling and even a few small wood blocks or logs were pushed home around the baby's feet in these weeks before Christmas.

A good relationship with the butcher resulted in a cow heel for a soup starter, and a kidney to augment our meat ration, meant that my cupboard was totally unlike Mother Hubbard's. It was far more exciting than any other Christmas shopping I have ever done.

Up went the garlands of paper chains, the trails of ivy and the sprigs of holly, while around a minute tree were our gifts to each other: a woolly ball for the babe, a few cigarettes for my husband; for in these days almost every adult smoked. There were books and magazines, a money gift for me and my mother's present of a Victorian-type rag rug to go before our open fire-grate.

But after lunch came near disaster. The baby was restless and fretful and what seemed a slight cold developed into a struggle for breath. His small face was waxy. He did not scream but his little fists clenched into tight balls. He refused to feed - air meant more to him than food. We were at our wits' end, for at the best of times doctors are often difficult to contact at Christmas time and we had no telephone - too many were on war service, and retirees were hard pressed.

Then we thought of the fire station. There was always someone on duty and they had that precious telephone. My husband ran to the station. There, used to any emergency during the war period, they sprang into action, and very soon a gentle, elderly doctor was with us.

"Not much we can do for such a small chap," he said, and my heart sank. "Let's try cuddling him! Hold him closely to your chest and warm him up. Let him feel your steady breathing and gently and regularly pat his back." He stayed a while, and I persevered with what he had suggested. Minutes seemed like hours while we waited for Nature to do its wonderful work. Then the breathing grew less painful and he eased into a quiet sleep. The asthma attack had passed.

As we sat quietly by the fire, with the babe sleeping peacefully in his cot, resting on the small mattress stuffed with straw which I had made for him, surely it was not unlike that very first Christmas of all?

A Dickensian Christmas

SCROOGE'S DEBATE WITH HIS NEPHEW FRED CONCERNING CHRISTMAS
from 'A Christmas Carol'

Once upon a time - of all the good days in the year, on Christmas Eve - old Scrooge sat busy in his counting-house. It was cold, bleak, biting weather; foggy withal; and he could hear the people in the court outside go wheezing up and down, beating their hands upon their breasts, and stamping their feet upon the pavement stones to warm them. The City clocks had only just gone three, but it was quite dark already - it had not been light all day - and candles were flaring in the windows of the neighbouring offices, like ruddy smears upon the palpable brown air. The fog came pouring in at every chink and keyhole, and was so dense without, that, although the court was of the narrowest, the houses opposite were mere phantoms. To see the dingy cloud come drooping down, obscuring everything, one might have thought that nature lived hard by, and was brewing on a large scale.

The door of Scrooge's counting-house was open, that he might keep his eye upon his clerk, who in a dismal little cell beyond, a sort of tank, was copying letters. Scrooge had a very small fire, but the clerk's fire

you! Much good it has ever done you!"

"There are many things from which I might have derived good, by which I have not profited, I dare say," returned the nephew; "Christmas among the rest. But I am sure I have always thought of Christmas-time, when it has come round - apart from the veneration due to its sacred name and origin, if anything belonging to it can be apart from that - as a good time; a kind, forgiving, charitable, pleasant time; the only time I know of, in the long calendar of the year, when men and women seem by one consent to open their shut-up hearts freely, and to think of people below them as if they really were fellow-passengers to the grave, and not another race of creatures bound on other journeys. And therefore, uncle, though it has never put a scrap of gold or silver in my pocket, I believe that it has done me good and will do me good, and I say, 'God bless it!' "

The clerk in the tank involuntarily applauded. Becoming immediately sensible of the impropriety, he poked the fire, and extinguished the last frail spark for ever.

"Let me hear another sound from you," said Scrooge, "and you'll keep your Christmas by losing your situation! You're quite a powerful speaker, sir," he added, turning to his nephew. "I wonder you don't go into Parliament."

"Don't be angry, uncle. Come! Dine with us tomorrow."

Scrooge said that he would see him - Yes, indeed he did. He went the whole length of the expression, and said that he would see him in that extremity first.

"But why?" cried Scrooge's nephew. "Why?"

"Why did you get married?" said Scrooge.

"Because I fell in love."

"Because you fell in love!" growled Scrooge, as if that were the only one thing in the world more ridiculous than a merry Christmas. "Good afternoon!"

"Nay, uncle, but you never came to see me before that happened. Why give it as a reason for not coming now?"

"Good afternoon," said Scrooge.

"I want nothing from you, I ask nothing of you , why cannot we be friends?"

"Good afternoon!" said Scrooge.

There never was such a goose. Bob said he didn't believe there ever was such a goose cooked. Its tenderness and flavour, size and cheapness, were the themes of universal admiration. Eked out by apple-sauce and mashed potatoes, it was sufficient dinner for the whole family; indeed, as Mrs Cratchit said with great delight (surveying one small atom of a bone upon the dish), they hadn't ate it all at last! Yet every one had had enough, and the youngest Cratchits in particular, were steeped in sage and onion to the eyebrows! But now, the plates being changed by Miss Belinda, Mrs Cratchit left the room alone - too nervous to bear witnesses - to take the pudding up and bring it in.

Suppose it should not be done enough! Suppose it should break in turning out! Suppose somebody should have got over the wall of the back-yard, and stolen it, while they were merry with the goose - a supposition at which the two young Cratchits became livid! All sorts of horrors were supposed.

Hallo! A great deal of steam! The pudding was out of the copper. A smell like a washing-day! That was the cloth. A smell like an eating-house and a pastrycook's next door to each other, with a laundress's next door to that! That was the pudding! In half a minute Mrs Cratchit entered - flushed, but smiling proudly - with the pudding, like a speckled cannon-ball, so hard and firm, blazing in half of half-a-quartern of ignited brandy, and bedight with Christmas holly stuck into the top.

Oh, a wonderful pudding! Bob Cratchit said, and calmly too, that he regarded it as the greatest success achieved by Mrs Cratchit since their marriage. Mrs Cratchit said that now the weight was off her mind, she would confess she had had her doubts about the quantity of flour. Everybody had something to say about it, but nobody said or thought it was at all a small pudding for a large family. It would have been flat heresy to do so. Any Cratchit would have blushed to hint at such a thing.

At last the dinner was all done, the cloth was cleared, the hearth swept, and the fire made up. The compound in the jug being tasted, and considered perfect, apples and oranges were put upon the table, and a shovel-full of chestnuts on the fire. Then all the Cratchit family drew round the hearth, in what Bob Cratchit called a circle, meaning half a one; and at Bob Cratchit's elbow stood the family display of glass. Two tumblers, and a custardcup without a handle. These held the hot stuff from

Now, the screaming had subsided, and faces were in a glow, and curls in a tangle, and Mr Pickwick, after kissing the old lady as before mentioned, was standing under the mistletoe, looking with a very pleased countenance on all that was passing around him, when the young lady with the black eyes, after a little whispering with the other young ladies, made a sudden dart forward, and, putting her arm round Mr Pickwick's neck saluted him affectionately on the left cheek; and before Mr Pickwick distinctly knew what was the matter, he was surrounded by the whole body, and kissed by every one of them.

It was a pleasant thing to see Mr Pickwick in the centre of the group, now pulled this way, and then that, and first kissed on the chin, and then on the nose, and then on the spectacles: and to hear the peals of laughter which were raised on every side; but it was a still more pleasant thing to see Mr Pickwick, blinded shortly afterwards with a silk handkerchief, falling up against the wall, and scrambling into corners, and going through all the mysteries of blind-man's buff, with the utmost relish for the game, until at last he caught one of the poor relations, and then had to evade the blind-man himself, which he did with a nimbleness and agility that elicited the admiration and applause of all beholders. The poor relations caught the people who they thought would like it, and, when the game flagged, got caught themselves. When they were all tired of blind-man's buff, there was a great game at snap-dragon, and when fingers enough were burned with that, and all the raisins were gone, they sat down by the huge fire of blazing logs to a substantial supper, and a mighty bowl of wassail, something smaller than an ordinary wash-house copper, in which the hot apples were hissing and bubbling with a rich look, and a jolly sound, that were perfectly irresistible.

"This," said Mr Pickwick, looking round him, "this is, indeed, comfort."

"Our invariable custom," replied Mr Wardle. "Everybody sits down with us on Christmas Eve, as you see them now - servants and all; and here we wait, until the clock strikes twelve, to usher Christmas in, and beguile the time with forfeits and old stories. Trundle, my boy, rake up the fire."

Up flew the bright sparks in myriads as the logs were stirred. The deep red blaze sent forth a rich glow, that penetrated into the furthest corner of the room, and cast its cheerful tint on every face.

A Wartime Christmas

THEY TIED A LABEL ON MY COAT
by Hilda Hollingsworth

Miss Hollingsworth's account of her own evacuation during the Second World War tells of four very different Christmases. Propaganda always described those children who had found homes better than their own, happy times filled with sunshine, and haymaking and full creamy milk, and snow and presents better than anything Mum could afford. But much of the reality went unrecorded, except in books such as this one. Here is an extract of Hilda's first Christmas - the only really happy one- where the two sisters awake to find that, although Mum may not have come, Santa had.

" 'Ild, 'Ild, Wake up! 'E's bin! Santa's bin! Come an' feel . . ."

Auntie had said we could switch on the light. Our woolly stockings bulged temptingly. Sticking out of the top of each was a celluloid doll with feathers stuck around waist and head. I delved inside. A rolled sheet of transfers. Picture colouring book. Paints, with names like Vermillion, Indigo and Yellow Ochre. A round wooden pillbox full of hundreds and thousands. A whip and top. Chocolate medal. A bright new penny. Then the apple and orange that today were just usual, and right deep inside the toe the three nuts which Mum always called Faith, 'Ope and Charity. I never knew why.

have one! But don't spoil your dinners." That's what was worrying me too. And I don't suppose Auntie ever knew that we really peeled our oranges just to get the smell.

A FARMHOUSE CHRISTMAS IN LONDON'S BLITZ
Anon

Gran had a big house; five bedrooms, eight steps leading up to the front door, and a huge cellar, which Grandpa had used as his workshop; he was a carpenter by trade. They brought up twelve children in that house. I suppose it didn't seem so big with all that lot, but with just the two of them it was a wonderful temporary home for me and the kids, especially with my husband away.

Anyway, we cleared away Grandpa's stuff in the cellar, and made quite a cosy den down there. Grandpa knocked up two sets of bunks for the kids in their own corner, and another set for him and Gran. I had a cosy little hole done like they used to have in Wales, where he'd been brought up with a sort of cupboard bed. We had a gas stove down there, but Gran preferred to use the old fired copper which Grandpa adapted for her. She wasn't happy about the gas being used. We spent most of our time down there during the blitz in fact. It got pretty dark though, as Grandpa had blocked up the window with sandbags against blast. We had lots of Tilley lamps, as there never had been electricity or gas lamps down there, and Grandpa needed plenty of light for his work. We were luckier than most I reckon, with our shelter comforts.

Grandpa had, with the help of a couple of neighbours, put up four huge beams going across the cellar and resting on the top of the bare brick and stone walls - to give a bit of extra protection in case of a direct hit he said. My poor little two up, two down didn't stand a chance, but Gran's house was made of much sterner stuff!

We decorated properly for Christmas down there, with jolly paper streamers and honeycomb pendants. The kids made loads of paper garlands which we had put all over the house! It kept them occupied for

ON THIS DAY
from 'Salute of the Guns'
by Donald Boyd

December 25th 1917

We had got two barrels of beer for the men, pork, cabbage, Christmas pudding, apples, oranges and nuts. These things had taken us three weeks to collect.

I was glad to think that after midday dinner I should begin my journey to the guns. I told Hampstead I should not ride. Nothing could be more pleasant on Christmas Day than to have this sort of holiday, to walk through the snow alone and undisturbed, and at the end of the journey to be greeted by friends. It was almost as good as though one walked out of the station at Grassington, leaving the village behind, and strode out on the road up to the cottage at Starbottom, knowing that the fires would be lit and the house full of merry people. Upon the dresser there would stand the enormous double-handled funnel which someone had presented as a challenge cup, standing in a treacle tin painted ebony black, and perhaps they might have pushed a cork into the funnel and turned it into a loving-cup. Meantime I plodded in the silent snow. The rucksack, full of late parcels, clung comfortably to my back. My box respirator bumped a little on my left side, my steel helmet on my right shoulder, and I swung my long Malacca trench-stick at my side. I wished the guns were even more than ten or twelve miles away as I walked along the empty road.

In front the black trunks of Havrincourt Wood rose from the snow, sheltering small corrugated huts, livid in the winter evening. The curls of grey smoke rose among the straight, bare timber to the darker sky. The huts were propped and patched in all manner of ways, draped raggedly with frosted sacking. I pursued my way on a ride through the wood as night fell, and after a little while a brilliant moon rose and threw upon the snow at either hand the grey shadows of the trees. A couple of infantrymen met me, walking with the raid shuffling gait which seemed to be induced by life in the trenches; shoulders bent, chins forward, steel helmets inclined to the ground, the feet at an angle of ninety degrees, and the rifle slung upon the

standing on a cloth of newspaper. A case of whisky was open on the floor. There was even a Christmas tree cut from the plantation.

"My hat, this is luxury!"

"Not 'arf, sir," Tanner said, "but it's nothing to what's coming."

Tanner had made *hors d'oeuvre* from two olives, a tin of sardines and the scrapings of a tin of bloater paste. Then there was turkey garnished with ham. After dinner the sergeants came down and settled in with the whisky.

SOJOURN IN THERESIENSTADT CHRISTMAS IN CAPTIVITY

from 'A Conspiracy of Decency - The Rescue of Danish Jews during World War II'
by Emmy E. Werner

Despite their constant fear and chronic hunger, some Danish prisoners still managed to celebrate Christmas Eve and the birthday of their Queen.
On December 25th, 1943, Ralph Oppenhejm wrote in his diary:

Yesterday afternoon when I left the barracks and returned "home" ....I saw one of the Holm daughters, sitting at the edge of her bed, her head bowed over a prayer book.

She did not hear me come, but sang with a shaky voice, "Silent Night, Holy Night" ...Yes, it was Christmas. No one among us had spoken about it - we all tried not to think about it. But it was Christmas; that could not be denied. "Silent night, Holy Night"... and tears ran down the face of Miss Holm... The nurse from our block came and told us that at six o'clock there would be a church service in the camp. Miss Holm took her coat and asked me if I would come along, so we both went to the Christmas service... Snow fell through the leaky roof and covered the faces of the people who had assembled. The room was filled to the rafters. There was an altar - a bed stand, covered with a blanket. On it was a huge primitive

PRISONER IN GERMANY
Adapted from 'Monica - a Heroine of the Danish Resistance'
by Christine Sutherland

As the days shortened and the long winter set in and bitter cold permeated the cells, Monica's strength began to ebb away. The long stint in West Prison, where each day she had expected to be led out and executed, and nearly six months in Cottbus were beginning to take their toll on a woman unaccustomed to hardship. Her indomitable spirit was unbroken, but physically she was now a shadow of herself. Only her huge, extraordinary eyes remained and the beautiful emaciated hands, reminiscent of Dürer's painting. Only one letter from home had so far reached her (mail was disrupted by the saturation bombing), a brief postcard on a Red Cross letter form. Finally in early December, two more letters arrived and two welcome parcels with cigarettes, a few clothes, toiletries, and the most desired article of all, real soap. She decided to start preparations for a Danish Christmas in prison.

There were now five Danish women in cell 12. Unlike Monica, the younger girls suffered more acutely from hunger than from cold and constantly fantasized about food. "I don't believe that one can ever imagine how much one thinks about food if one is forever hungry," recalled Pia. "Tulle and I kept listing the delicious things we would eat when we finally got home. We agreed that after we had been with the family for a while, we would go down to Mrs. Wichfeld's (Monica's) estate near Maribo, where we would each lie on a soft, clean bed and be served one delicious course after another... In the meantime, we had to be content with slices of rye bread, which contained more sawdust than rye, a thin soup, and occasionally a few potatoes which we ate hungrily, skin and all... I don't want to advertise Macleans toothpaste, but it tastes quite good spread on bread, if you are hungry enough!"

A week before Christmas the girls were sent to work in the local gas-mask factory on a 7a.m. to 7p.m. shift. Monica stayed behind. She busied herself cleaning the cell and making it as homely as possible for Christmas, a tough assignment. She managed to make a tablecloth out of white paper napkins from her home parcels and cut out small, beautiful red

We can only imagine what Monica's thoughts may have been that night. She well knew that her life was ebbing away. Only a few stitches remained in the tapestry of her life.

An Essex
Christmas

SNOW FIGHTS
by Spike Mays

Spike Mays was born in 1907 at a hamlet near the village of Ashdon in north-west Essex. In 1969 his book 'Reuben's Corner' was published, from which the following extract is taken; a sequel, 'Return to Anglia', appeared in 1986. Both books are, as 'The Times Literary Supplement' said, a continuous cascade of anecdotes.

In the winter months our return journey from school was often in total darkness. There were no street or road lights and the stars would not be out until much later. If there was snow or ice on the roads and fields we would be late home. Not because we were unable to negotiate the roads but because we would make slides, toboggan runs, snowmen, and would have long, fierce snow-fights. In the snow-fighting there were often minor casualties. The big boys, the cunning ones who had seen a winter or two, used to cheat. They would press and press their snowballs until they were almost blocks of ice. Sometimes they would even slip a small stone into a soft snowball. There would be cut cheeks, blood on the snow and other fights - fiercer fights - without snow. Each End would challenge other

Ends and Bartlow Hamlet to make the longest and most slippery slide in the road. Some were longer than cricket pitches but it was great fun to see the glowing cheeks, to hear the shrieks of joy and laughter as novices fell on their backsides. And when we had had enough or were getting hungry we would cover the long slides with snow so that no one could see them, hoping to see old men fall on them and curse like mad.

The toboggan runs were made on the steep slope of Hilly Meadow, behind Cobby Webb's farm, or Chapel Farm, to give it its right title. We made our own toboggans or sledges from boxes scrounged from old Vic Eason, the village shopkeeper - father of Reg, Mabel Eason's husband. If Bill Smith the blacksmith was not too busy making great iron shoes for the Suffolk Punches and Clydesdales, or was not bent in two with his crippling rupture, he would put iron runners on a sledge for sixpence. Then off we would go to Hilly Meadow, sometimes in total darkness to whip down the steep slopes like lightning. A small stream ran along the bottom of Hilly Meadow. On its bank there was a great hawthorn hedge, quite ten feet high. If the sledges were overloaded, or we did not put out our feet quickly enough to do some useful braking, we would tear through the hawthorn hedge and land in the stream. Inevitably there would be casualties here, too, mostly gashed cheeks from the hawthorn spikes, ripped clothing or a total immersion in icy water.

CAROL SINGING
by Spike Mays

This is another extract from 'Reuben's Corner'. Eventually 'Reuben's Corner' and Essex were left behind and Spike Mays was 'Away to Canterbury, the army, and a life that would never be the same again'.

At Christmas it was a different matter. Most of the choir, and sometimes Bartlow Hamlet only, would band together for carol singing. We would walk miles and miles through the deepest drifts, to all the Ends, singing louder and longer than we ever did at church.

For this we made our own lanterns - jam jars with candles, of which we each had one. Usually a dozen or more of us would set out, all jam-jarred and collector-boxed. Muffs, helmets, scarves, winter-warmers and leggings made from old sacks were the garments we wore to keep out the cold. People could see us for miles before they heard us for our lights were easily discerned in a largely lightless land. It must have looked a pretty straggling torchlight procession from the distant view but close up we no doubt looked much better and more Christmassy - all red of cheek, our frosty breath blowing into the air pinked and yellowed by the candlelight. Farmers were the best payers - Tilbrooks, Furzes, Haggers and Webbs. Usually they would invite us in, particularly if they had been at the bottle, to sing to them in the warm, and we would then get silver instead of copper plus mince pies and lovely yellow apples, the latter all mellow and brown-pippy through ripening on oat straw in lofts. Now and again they would give us wine and small beer. The wine was all right because it warmed us up but the small beer made our teeth chatter and our voices quiver.

Sometimes we used to cheat a bit by not singing the proper words.

Beer by the pailful, makes us gay, triumphant,
Bring some, ye citizens of Steventon's End.
Fetch out the mince pies, hot and sweet and ta-sty;
If you don't we'll bash your door in;
We'll bash your silly door in;
We'll bash your silly door in,
As sure as we're born.

We only sang such words to those who were too mean to open the door. If we sang one word wrong inside a house the news would go round the village and the parson would tick us off for not doing the job properly.

Old Johnny Purkis came with us one night. He couldn't sing a bit, nor could he do the church job he had as well as it should have been done. Johnny was the organ blower. Many a time he let Mabel Eason down by not pumping when wind was required. He would sit in a little recess at the back of the organ all by himself, screened from the congregation by green curtains. Mabel would know the moment he arrived, for he would swish the curtains closed with a great flourish, making the brass rings dance and jingle on their rail. From that moment she had to hope for the best.

Sometimes he would drop off to sleep and the organ would groan and splutter to a stop in the middle of a hymn or psalm. Sometimes he would snore, or make the loudest of rude noises and the churchwarden would nip smartly round to tell him off and ginger him up.

We took him carol singing because he was the best man in Essex for walking straight in snow and could lead the way. This was curious because when roads were clear he would lurch from side to side - as though completely without control of his spindly legs. In this day and age old Johnny would not have lasted ten seconds.

Between Christmas and the New Year there was always a spate of choral and bell-ringing practice. On one occasion the Reverend Hartley had got a bit frosty over something or other and had doubled practice nights to two per week. Rumour had it that Starchy Williams had complained and advised that we choirboys should be gingered up. With that end in view we were ordered to report to the parish church where the campanologists were ringing out wild bells to the wild sky - instead of to the Sunday school building. There was plenty of flying cloud and several degrees of frost on that wintry night - enough to crisp the top of a thick blanket of snow.

Poddy Coote, the leading choir boy, thereupon hatched a plot. When everybody else was wending their way to home and fireside, there was one who was not. Lo and behold, it was Starchy. By some unaccountable circumstance he found himself alone . . . locked in the belfry.

And when all the Christian folk of Ashdon had gone upstairs; were on their knees a-saying prayers - including the Reverend Hartley - a sound rang through the wintry night. One wild bell alone was ringing to the wild sky. It was not the customary steady toll, more of a feverish clanging.

When the Reverend Hartley arrived at the church, after plodding through half a mile of deep snow drifts, to let Starchy loose, he had to make the same trip all over again - twice. He had forgotten the key.

"Retribushun!" said the leading choir boy. "That's what it were, retribushun!"

He may have been right. Anyway, the choir practices were halved forthwith.

SIREN NIGHT AND SILENT NIGHT
by Brian Mellish

Brian Mellish was born in 1940 at Dagenham. His house was in the last street of Metropolitan Essex. Beyond lay a huge cornfield and in the middle distance the wooded hills running up to Lambourne End could be seen: Hainault Forest, remnant of the vast Essex Forest of the Middle Ages. He now farms at Mautby in Norfolk.

The first Christmas I can remember is the one of 1944. My sister, Sheila, three years older than I, had with my help - if help it could be called - spent many evenings cutting strips of coloured paper which she had gathered from various sources. The strips of paper were then pasted together to form chains which were now festooned in the kitchen and sitting room. Paper bells, coloured balls, were hung about the pictures of Harlequin and Columbine which hung in our living room. Sprigs of holly - illegally obtained on our last visit to the Forest - were tucked behind the chiming clock and the pair of china dogs on the mantelshelf which were half-hidden by a number of Christmas cards.

Before teatime on Christmas Eve I accompanied Sheila on her visits to her friends when they exchanged small homemade gifts. Our last call was to June Nelson, a special friend of Sheila's, who lived opposite to us. As we left, she followed us out into the street and pointed to the darkening sky. Looking eastwards, she said, "Look for the moving star over Bethlehem." We all looked, two seven-year-old girls and a four-year-old boy. We all saw the star.

That night, in the east, there were lights of a different kind. "Go to sleep," said Mother. "It's only God's fireworks." But Mother's tense body and the earlier sound of sirens told us that those 'fireworks' were an air raid, probably on nearby Hornchurch Airfield.

Despite the air raid, the excitement and anticipation of Christmas had tired us and we were soon asleep. In Mother's bed, as always on such nights when the siren wailed. I suppose she thought it better that we should all go or survive together.

We knew nothing until we awoke next morning. Not in Mother's bed but in the living room where there was already a blazing fire. Mother had carried us there during the raid and put us in a makeshift bed surrounded by a wire mesh frame supporting on its top a thick sheet of steel; our indoor air raid shelter.

At the foot of this bed and hanging on a hook that also held our gas masks there were, not stockings, but pillow cases, bulging, even though it was a time of austerity. Sheila and I gasped and fell on these cornucopias. First there was a small mesh stocking containing an apple, an orange and some cobnuts. A colouring book with a picture of a lion on the cover. A little wooden man, fixed on a frame, which did all manner of gyrations and acrobatics when the string attached to his body was pulled. (This toy had been made by my grandfather.) Then a set of cardboard skittles; a magnificent grey battleship bristling with panel pin guns (made by George Wright, our neighbour next door, from offcuts of wood gleaned while repairing bomb damaged houses). Next came newly knitted gloves, hats and a pullover in Fair Isle pattern. My sister had a china doll which she seemed to like and which to my mind made a noise more like a bleating sheep than a baby.

There were also skipping ropes, whipping tops, bouncing balls, sets of five stones and my first box of marbles. These last presents were very important in the lives of children. These simple pieces of equipment would keep us occupied in the backyard or in the street all the year round. I suppose we were the last generation of children to inherit the culture of street games which had been handed down for centuries. Skipping; either by one girl on her own or, with a long rope stretched across the street, with half-a-dozen boys and girls and this was always accompanied by a chant. Hopscotch was played by chalking squares on the pavement stones. Small groups played five stones or marbles, a girl alone would bounce a ball or juggle one, two or three balls in the air.

After we had opened our presents and dressed in front of the fire, the wireless was switched on and after it had warmed up it was tuned for us to hear the Christmas Bells.

We all had a letter from my father who was serving in the army in Algeria. My letter consisted of some drawings of aeroplanes and ships and a little note which had to be read to me. It took pride of place on the mantelshelf.

Christmas dinner; what a feast! Roast potatoes, parsnips, Brussels sprouts, and carrots all grown by Mother on her allotment, and rabbit stuffed with sage and onions. In the summer it was my sister's and my job to gather food for the rabbits; dandelions (which stained our hands), sow thistles, cow parsley and grass by the sackful. In the winter the rabbits had to make do with the trimmings of greens from the greengrocer, a little hay, and household scraps mixed with bran.

Our Christmas pudding was date pudding with a sprig of holly on the top.

After dinner we played with our new toys on the luxurious new peg mat. Mother had been working hard for several months making this mat, with Christmas as her deadline. It was no ordinary rag mat. Somehow she had managed to obtain some thick yarn which she then dyed into different colours before cutting up. We had all helped, especially with cutting it into small lengths ready for the ties. I had even used the special peg to push the yarn through the canvas backing and then to knot the yarn. No doubt my efforts had to be unpicked and re-done after I had gone to bed. To us, on this Christmas Day, our carpet which must have been at least three yards square, was as good as the best Wilton.

Our really special present, which was from Father, had yet to be opened; it had been saved for our afternoon delight. Mother removed the wrapping paper to uncover a box on which were pictured clusters of exotic fruits; apricots, figs.... She opened the box. A puff of blue smoke arose. Was this some magic from the mystic east? No, the crystallised fruits for which poor Father had saved his meagre allowance were just blue-green mouldy puff-balls.

"Never mind, let's have some lemonade and hazel nuts," said Mother, "they'll be just as nice." But oh, how she would have liked to have tasted just one apricot. The slight quiver in the corner of Mother's mouth belied her cheerfulness. She was, no doubt, wondering how to break the news to Father and imagining his disappointment.

Tea was an effort, as Christmas tea always is, but trifle and iced Christmas cake could not be refused.

After tea the lights were turned off and the three of us sat round the fire and sang carols. Was Father, the father I could not remember, sitting round a fire in the desert singing carols? We liked to think so.

There were no sirens, no air raids; it was a quiet night.

TEA PARTY
an extract from 'Most Happy Husbandman',
by Ethelind Fearon, published in 1946

Marian has been concocting the essentials for a Christmas tree. All the boiled eggs for weeks have been opened with delicate precision and treasured like Dresden china. More so. When there were sufficient for her purpose she painted them from a motley collection of little tins which held repulsive oddments of bright enamel, gold paint and hideous orange lacquer. With a bright string hung through the end they are tied, open end downwards, to the Christmas tree and look like fairy-tale bells, all little dabs of purple and blue and gold merged in rainbow hues.

The enemy has been kind enough to shower us with bushels of tinfoil in streamers, a gift straight from heaven which is eagerly collected and hung in dingle-dangles from the ends of the branches, although probably not intended for that purpose.

The tree itself is a beautiful young fir dug up from the plantation, roots and all, and planted in a huge flower pot. After Twelfth Night it will be carefully replanted in its old place to dig in its toes again and go on growing. It looks lovely when Jonathan has been called in to fix the electric lights, which twinkle like incandescent appendices in red and green. Spreading its dark arms against the panelling it bears the silvered icicles of German foil dripping from bough to bough, and little shimmery globes of many-coloured fire which were our breakfast eggs a week or two ago.

This time there will be no present for Samuel the cat. Last year we tied a chicken leg on the topmost branch for him, alongside the fairy, and on Christmas eve he climbed up while the house was sleeping and stole it prematurely.

Marian says he's so pretty when he steals (with an absentminded air, and both eyes shut) that she is obliged to forgive him anything, even her breakfast kidney. It is perhaps as well that we have no women judges if that is their outlook on thieving.

The last of the ploughing is done and the earth left to the elements for the final breaking-down. The last leaf has fallen, and rooks cluster like black pears in the topmost branches of the naked elms.

Draining, ditching, threshing and a dozen other jobs are under way. People say, "What can anyone find to *do* in the country in the winter."

If you're producing something - anything - there is always enough to do. The country is never dull, although a dull mind can make it so.

We work. And when work is done we rest. We eat and drink and talk and go to bed. Some of us get born and a few of us die. And that's all. It doesn't sound a lot and yet somehow put together it is a lifetime, and if we've missed anything we don't notice it.

Every December, just before Christmas, we organise a teaparty in the village hall for the old age pensioners. There is a Christmas tree with some kind of little present for everyone, and such a profusion of cakes, jellies, mince pies, sausage rolls and blancmanges that a stranger would suppose we were entertaining refugees.

After tea they always have a concert to which anyone in the village may come by paying a shilling as they walk in, a similar amount being handed to each ancient on going out, so that the two processes more or less cancel out.

The programme is much as usual this year. Tea at half-past five, presents handed down from the tree by Sandy, thinly disguised as Father Christmas, at half-past six, concert at seven.

Marian as usual is at the piano, an ancient upright with the peculiar hollow tinkle common to pianos in village halls. She dearly loves a tune, the commoner the better, and can play anything with equal ease either facing the piano or looking over her shoulder to see if the singer is going through the chorus three times or only twice. Besides, she knows where the three dumb notes are and can dodge them, whereas a better player might be completely flummoxed by such a trivial deficiency. I have noticed that the more one is an expert, the more easily is he confounded by the unexpected obtrusion of the primitive.

I am, as usual, the Man who Moves Things, a handyman, lurking in the dark recesses behind the stage, to produce tables and chairs as required, disgorge cutlery for the inevitable Stage Breakfast, tend the slightly intractable curtain, and be there when wanted, but otherwise as far out of the way as possible.

Talent is strictly parochial, the same old performers singing the same old songs they have done these many years. Any innovation would be slightly disconcerting to the audience who would feel that they were being left behind and couldn't join in.

Mrs Potton has volunteered to sing, a proceeding which I regard with some misgiving, fearing that she may introduce an over-opulent note into an entirely domestic atmosphere. But even though I doubt her wisdom I cannot refuse the offer.

Boy George is the only performer from the farm. He renders 'Land of Hope and Glory' on a cornet with slightly too much spit and a certain amount of groping for top notes, but stays the course nobly, and finishes up with a burst of speed and loud acclamations from the multitude in the body of the hall.

Tiny Caton need only be himself. Wearing his grandfather's smock, buskins, beaver hat and red handkerchief, he sings farming songs, to the glory of the naïve nature and essential shrewdness of the Essex labourer.

His dialect is superb, his make-up just bucolic enough and not too much. I could listen to him for hours. It's funny all right, uproariously funny, but it's more than that, there's something elemental about it that goes right to the heart of the labouring life.

He is succeeded by our comedy trio, whose sketch the audience know so well that they join in. If a player goes astray they render kindly assistance.

Voice from the rear, "Old 'ard a minnit, Jack, you've forgot the bit about the burnt saussage."

"Right you are, boy," says Jack from the stage, "I bin an' forgot it agin same as usual. Thank yer from me." And he knuckles his forehead in gratitude, goes back to pick up the dropped line, and proceeds smoothly on his way again.

Two girls sing a duet. One of them, stricken dumb in the middle of the verse, can do nothing but coyly search the corners of the ceiling for inspiration, one leg wrapped round the other and hands behind back in an agony of shyness, while the other valiantly carries on, but in the second verse her mate revives somewhat and gets through half of it without moving her mouth, a marvellous feat.

Mrs Potton is the next performer. From my peephole in the back curtain I can't quite see her as she walks on, but the cheering and stamping surprise me considerably. I had not believed her to be so popular.

And then the reason becomes apparent. Ample of architecture, and florid of hue, she struts the stage in an extravagant paraphrase of bull-fighting attire. Black satin breeches caress her ample thighs, a scarlet cummerbund and yellow blouse delineate her convexity all too unkindly, a broad black felt crowns saucily her coal black curls, and behind the left ear lurks a paper rose.

I am deprived of half the effect, but if the front view is anything like as funny as the rear she is doing pretty well. The audience laps it up and will not be quiet, and I instantly revoke all my previous decisions about her. If she is human enough to make of herself a Roman holiday for the assembled ancients, God bless her, she'll do!

But, presently, by much waving of an over-diamonded hand, she achieves silence, and explains with a kind of pained resignation that she isn't funny at all. She is a bull-fighter who loves a little gipsy, and is going to sing a song about it.

A Country Christmas

BRING IN THE HOLLY

This extract is taken from 'The Scythe in the Apple Tree', by C. Henry Warren published in 1953. The author had been living in a thatched cottage called Timbers just outside Finchingfield for the last sixteen years.

It was Christmas Eve, and during the afternoon I went to see my friends at Thurstons Farm. A milky fog hid the countryside, where the only sound was of small water-drops dripping from hedge and tree. Everything was unnaturally still - attentive, or so it seemed, to something not yet audible to the human ear.

I had not met a soul all the way; and then, just as I was nearing the farm, suddenly, as if from nowhere, Dave Johnson appeared, followed by his three goats. With his hands stuck in his trousers pockets, leaving the long wrists showing bare, and his jacket collar pulled up round his chin, Dave walked slowly, silently, along the grass verge; and his goats stepped daintily beside him, shaking the peeled sticks which he has slung round their necks to prevent them (only they do not) from straying into people's yards and gardens.

"A merry Christmas." Dave shouted and at once disappeared, goats and all, like a desert shepherd passing in the mists.

There was silence again, heavy and wet and lonely.

And then it was old Ernie who appeared, just as mysteriously, his smiling face framed in the fog as he peered over the garden hedge. Soon he was joined by his wife, neat and trim as ever.

"A merry Christmas to you, sir!" she said, for she has an old-fashioned courtesy, a gentility, rare in the countryside these days. And then, holding out a small paper parcel, she added: "If you are going round to the farm, I wonder if you would mind taking this to the lady?"

At the farm itself the same wish greeted me through the open kitchen door. Mrs Jackson was busy over the stove, cooking the Christmas delicacies, and Eddie was washing his weekly collection of ducks' eggs in the sink, ready for the eggman (as he is called) to take to the Packing Station. It was the sign of their friendly acceptance of me that they did not for a moment pause in their tasks. I shook the drops from my coat and sat down.

Outside the windows nothing was visible except the grey dusk of the fog; but a farm-house kitchen declares itself for what it is without the aid of a view over barn and byre, field and corn stack. It is the focus of the life of the farmstead; always there is some activity; always there is somebody coming or going. For fruitful friendliness I would choose Thurstons kitchen above any other I know. And so it was now. The spirit could not help blossoming in such a place - and perhaps especially on Christmas Eve.

Presently the farmer himself came in, the faithful spaniel at his heels. His eyebrows glistened with fog, his boots were covered with mud, there was the smell of cattle in his clothes.

"A merry Christmas!" he said, and well enough one could hear that he meant it to the full.

A merry Christmas - it is the word they all use here, the unashamed old greeting of the season which Englishmen have spoken through the centuries until lack of faith and excess of commercial enterprise have at last rendered it all but meaningless. But it is not meaningless to these people living miles from anywhere, remote from any centre but that of their own quiet, fertile lives. Merry they say and merry they mean: never mind what greeting others may use to-day.

... I made my way home at length, loaded with the gifts that had accompanied the simple wishes. The fog was clearing a little now and the true twilight descending. I came past an occasional cottage, with its paper decorations gaudy in the naked lamplight; past a week-ender's house, with its discreet crimson shades over the candles on the tea-table; past old George, shuffling along the lane, pushing a pile of Christmas wood on his rickety trolley. I set the presents on the table. A bottle of home-made mead; some Bramley apples, newly taken from a clamp in the garden, crisp and firm as the day they were picked; a pat of Jersey butter and a jam jar of cream; a sackful of holly in berry. What essential country presents they were, seeming to give so much more than themselves! And how eloquently they spoke of their givers - old Ernie and Dave, Mrs Jackson and the rest!

Under the ivy-twined beams that night and the bright red berries shining in the lamplight, I sat before the fire, when everybody else had gone to bed, listening to a recorded broadcast of the afternoon Carol Service from King's Chapel, Cambridge.

Double creatures that we are, pagan and Christian at one and the same time! We hang up the holly and the ivy, the yew and the mistletoe, in token, although we no longer acknowledge it, of the woodland gods, the woodland spirits, that ask to be taken indoors for a respite from the winter weather, to repay us for our kindness, who knows how, through the years to come. And then, sitting under their green shine, we join with heart, if not, these days, with voice, in the old carols that tell of a child who from His bed in the meagre straw smiled on the dark world He had come to lighten with His love.

Listening to the pure-toned voices of the boys as they sang those simple tunes of Christmas and to the experienced voices, full of character, of the men as they read the story of that long-ago birthday in Bethlehem, I thanked the inventors who had made it possible for me thus to span the miles and to bring back lost time at the mere twisting of a knob.

While I had been on my way up to the farm in the foggy afternoon, and Dave had gone by with his train of goats, and old Ernie's gentle wife had leaned over the hedge to ask me to take her Christmas gift to 'the lady', this Carol Service had been echoing under the vaulted roof of King's Chapel, where the still candle-flames shone on the age-black oak, and the Tudor roses blossomed enduringly in stone; but science had found the trick of capturing the winged sounds, and passed it on to me, so that I might loosen them on the air again to-night, here in the quiet room.

When the last Amen had died away and in the midnight silence I could hear only the small cracklings of the burning wood on the hearth, I sat on awhile in the still house thinking over the words I had been listening to. From the mantelpiece I took down the Christmas poem a friend had sent me:

> . . . Yes! And this is your house we cheer,
> Cheer this singular night;
> Our breath smokes well upon midnight air;
> Look out of window and find our light;
> Only a stable lantern still,
> Lit by a candle small and clear;
> And we sing, Peace, to men of goodwill.
> Does any such man live here?

I opened the window and leaned out into the solemn, breathing darkness. From down in the village, carried to me on the thick, wet air, came the pealing of the church bells. 'A merry Christmas,' I said in my heart, 'and Peace, to men of goodwill!'

A COUNTRY DOCTOR'S CHRISTMAS, 1930
by Geoffrey Barber

Dr Geoffrey Barber was in practice at Dunmow and High Easter from 1930 until his retirement in 1963. His book, 'Country Doctor', was published in 1973.

The prevalent illnesses differed in many ways from those which we meet today. Broadly, they were due to poverty and deficiency, whereas nowadays they are more likely to be caused by affluence and excess. The old people, and parents and children in large families, tended to be short of food, badly clothed, and poorly housed in damp old cottages with no drains. It was all very picturesque in summertime, roses and honeysuckle round the door and thatch on the roof - but the artists who drew these cottages for the Christmas calendars did not see the dripping leaks and the rat infested walls, the weeds and the litter in the cold winter months. There was one of these isolated cottages which has now been demolished, and which I had to visit on my first Christmas Day. Old Dr Tench had died on the night before, so a kind friend asked me to share his Christmas lunch with his growing family: and it was from that cheerful atmosphere that I went out in the cold snowy afternoon as dusk came on. It was a long, low thatched cottage with a brick path round it, and when I knocked on the door a little girl of about eight came and let me in. Her entire clothing was a cut down shirt of her father's, and I remember her blue little feet on the cold snow-dusted brick. In the downstairs room there were several children huddled round the table on which there was the end of a loaf, a jam pot and a pot of tea. I was taken upstairs to the tiny bedroom, where the mother lay in bed with her latest child of a week old, she told me she was suffering from 'milk fever'; by her side was her husband desperately ill with pneumonia, and there was a small fire in the grate from which the children had been sent downstairs when I came up.

As I was going out I asked the little girl what she had had to eat that day, and she said: "Oh, just bread and jam."

It is nice to think that that family not only survived, but the girls were attractive, married well and made good wives, and gave their elderly parents an extremely comfortable old age.

I have another memory of that first Christmas in 1930 in the small country community I have described, where much real poverty existed. Charity is a word that is not liked nowadays, but most of what I saw was spontaneous and Christian. Many of the well-to-do regarded it as a duty to old servants or tenants or neighbours, especially at Christmas time, when it was the custom to take round Christmas parcels. These were made up carefully to match the wants of the families: food, clothing, sweets and even small toys.

Dr Tench was dying, but he had nurses in the house. The domestic work of the house was all done by servants, so that Mrs Tench and her sisters would spend long days making up these parcels for the doctor's poor patients who were either on the Parish, or in his dispensary. If they were reasonably near, the parcels would be strapped precariously on the carriers of their bicycles and they would wheel them out, stop for a chat and bicycle home.

But most of the poorer patients were in the villages round: old worn out labourers, widows, or large families on pitifully low wages or with a sick wage earner 'on the club'. These were my job, and my car was loaded up according to the routine round of the day. Mondays and Thursdays were out at High Easter where I ate a picnic lunch in the surgery, returning through the Roothings. Tuesdays and Fridays were out to Takeley, and sometimes Hatfield Broad Oak, with Felsted in the afternoons and sometimes Broxted and Thaxted as well.

A few of the parcels were enormously heavy and included a single huge lump of coal. The best coal was delivered in really large pieces, and it was the job of the gardener's boy to break these up to a reasonable size: but around Christmas time Mrs Tench would go down to the cellar with sticky labels and put the names of families on appropriate lumps, which were brought up and delivered by me. I grumbled at first but was ashamed when I saw the genuine gratitude in the cottages.

CHRISTMAS IN A VILLAGE
by John Clare

Each house is swept the day before,
And windows stuck with evergreens;
The snow is besomed from the door,
And comfort crowns the cottage scenes.
Gilt holly with its thorny pricks
And yew and box with berries small,
These deck the unused candlesticks,
And pictures hanging by the wall.

Neighbours resume their annual cheer,
Wishing with smiles and spirits high
Glad Christmas and a happy year
To every morning passer-by.
Milkmaids their Christmas journeys go
Accompanied with favoured swain,
And children pace the crumping snow
To taste their granny's cake again.

Hung with the ivy's veining bough,
The ash trees round the cottage farm
Are often stripped of branches now
The cottar's Christmas hearth to warm.
He swings and twists his hazel band,
And lops them off with sharpened hook,
And oft brings ivy in his hand
To decorate the chimney nook . . .

The shepherd now no more afraid
Since custom doth the chance bestow
Starts up to kiss the giggling maid
Beneath the branch of mistletoe
That 'neath each cottage beam is seen
With pearl-like berries shining gay,
The shadow still of what hath been
Which fashion yearly fades away.

And singers too, a merry throng,
At early morn with simple skill
Yet imitate the angel's song
And chant their Christmas ditty still;
And 'mid the storm that dies and swells
By fits - in hummings softly steals
The music of the village bells
Ringing round their merry peals.

SKETCH BOOK
by Washington Irving

The snow seldom lingers for long in Britain and as it melts the colouring of the gradually revealed fields is emphasized. A walk on Christmas day such as that taken by Washington Irving with his host, the squire, always has a leisured quality about it. The 'business' of the world draws to a halt and everyone, both rich and poor, enjoys a sense of universal goodwill.

The beauty of the day was of itself sufficient to inspire philanthropy. Notwithstanding the frostiness of the morning, the sun in his cloudless journey had acquired sufficient power to melt away the thin covering of snow from every southern declivity, and to bring out the living green which adorns an English landscape even in mid-winter. Large tracts of smiling verdure contrasted with the dazzling whiteness of the shaded slopes and hollows. Every sheltered bank, on which the broad rays rested, yielded its silver rill of cold and limpid water, glittering through the dripping grass; and sent up slight exhalations to contribute to the thin haze that hung just above the surface of the earth. There was something truly cheering in this triumph of warmth and verdure over the frosty thraldom of winter; it was, as the squire observed, an emblem of Christmas hospitality, breaking through the chills of ceremony and selfishness, and thawing every heart into a flow. He pointed with pleasure to the indications of good cheer reeking from the chimneys of the comfortable farmhouses, and low thatched cottages. "I love," said he, "to see this day well kept by rich and poor; it is a great thing to have one day in the year, at least, when you are sure of being welcome wherever you go, and of having, as it were, the world all thrown open to you."

LARK RISE TO CANDLEFORD
by Flora Thompson

Christmas Day passed very quietly. The men had a holiday from work and the children from school and the churchgoers attended special Christmas services. Mothers who had young children would buy them an orange each and a handful of nuts; but, except at the end house and the inn, there was no hanging up of stockings, and those who had no kind elder sister or aunt in service to send them parcels got no Christmas presents.

Still, they did manage to make a little festival of it. Every year the farmer killed an ox for the purpose and gave each of his men a joint of beef, which duly appeared on the Christmas dinner-table together with plum pudding - not Christmas pudding, but suet duff with a good sprinkling of raisins. Ivy and other evergreens (it was not a holly country) were hung from the ceiling and over the pictures; a bottle of homemade wine was uncorked, a good fire was made up, and, with doors and windows closed against the keen, wintry weather, they all settled down by their own firesides for a kind of super-Sunday. There was little visiting of neighbours and there were no family reunions, for the girls in service could not be spared at that season, and the few boys who had gone out in the world were mostly serving abroad in the Army.

There were still bands of mummers in some of the larger villages, and village choirs went carol-singing about the countryside; but none of these came to the hamlet, for they knew the collection to be expected there would not make it worth their while. A few families, sitting by their own firesides, would sing carols and songs; that, and more and better food and a better fire than usual, made up their Christmas cheer.

A Children's Christmas

CHRISTMAS THROUGH A KNOTHOLE
by Katharine Gibson

Old Hans was the best wood carver in all the land. But just three weeks before Christmas, he was thrown into jail! Again and again he had been told not to hunt in the King's own hunting ground. But Hans's mouth would water for the taste of roast rabbit, and to the King's lands he would go and set his traps. This time, alas, Hans was caught.

The jailer was a kind man. Since Hans was old, he let him have a fire and some wood to carve. But Hans was very unhappy. To be in jail at Christmas, when all the village was making merry!

Hans lived all alone, but he had a good friend named Gretchen. Gretchen was seven years old and had big grey eyes and long, smooth yellow hair in two pig-tails. Gretchen also had a little brother named Max. He was as round and brown as she was pink and white. He was as naughty and full of laughter as she was quiet and thoughtful.

"Oh, Max," Gretchen said to her brother, "what shall we do? Poor

Uncle Hans is in jail, just for hunting rabbits. He always has his Christmas dinner with us. Now he won't have any - not a bite."

"And worse than that," said Max, "we won't get any toys!" For every year, of course, Old Hans carved the most wonderful toys for them. Max looked cross. Gretchen looked sad. They walked past the jail. Like all the other houses in the village, it was made of wood. The walls were very thick, and the only window was far, far above their heads.

Suddenly Max said, "Look, there is a hole."

It was a large knothole in the wood. Max stood on his tiptoes and put his eye to the hole. "I can see him. I can see Old Hans. He is carving, just the way he always does!"

"Oh, Max, let me see!" cried Gretchen.

She bent down, and sure enough she could see Old Hans - or part of him.

Max took out his pocket knife (every boy in the village carried a knife) and scratched at the hole until he made it bigger. Then he put his lips to the hole and called. "Hans, Uncle Hans, come here! Come to the knothole!"

Old Hans was surprised. He got up and followed the sound of the excited small voice. The children told him all the village news. In turn, he told them how long the days were in jail.

"It will be a sad Christmas for you, Uncle Hans," said Gretchen. "We will miss you at home."

"For us it will be even worse." Max was almost crying. "We won't have any toys - not one!"

"You come back here tomorrow," Uncle Hans said.

The children could hardly wait for the next day. In the morning, they hurried back to the knothole. "Here we are, here we are, Uncle Hans," they shouted.

The knothole was bigger now. Out of it, Uncle Hans pushed a tiny wooden figure. It was a little boy carrying a flower in his hand.

"Oh," cried Max, "it is just like me!"

"Only you never carry flowers," said Gretchen. "You just carry big sticks."

The next day, a fat duck came through the knothole. Then a market woman.

"Why," said Gretchen, "that is old Martha!"

Day after day, the tiny carved figures came through the knothole. At last the children had a whole village. And not one toy was more than three inches high.

"Uncle Hans has done so much for us," said Gretchen. "I wonder, can we make him a knothole Christmas dinner?"

They talked with their mother. And this is what they did. They wrapped some fine pieces of roast goose into long thin bundles, four of them. They took some long thin sausages that Hans liked ever so much. Gretchen baked some rolls. They were a very funny shape, not very different from the sausages, long and thin. Even the Christmas cakes were rolled up tight, with sugar and nuts inside.

"And a tall thin candle - a Christmas candle. I will make it myself," said Max. And he did.

Christmas Eve came. There was snow on the pointed roofs of the houses, and on the pointed tops of the fir trees. Just as the lights were lit, Max and Gretchen went to the jail.

They called Old Hans. He came and gave them the prettiest toy of all. It was a funny, fat little fellow with a star on his head - a Christmas angel. Then Max pushed, and Gretchen pushed, and soon Hans's Christmas dinner was inside the jail. Last of all, Max pushed through the candle.

"Made it myself!" he said proudly, jumping up and down.

The children said they had never had such toys, never. And they loved them because they were so tiny. And Hans said the best dinner he ever had was the Christmas dinner through a knothole.

THE NIGHT BEFORE CHRISTMAS
by Clement C. Moore

'Twas the night before Christmas, when all through the house
Not a creature was stirring, not even a mouse;
The stockings were hung by the chimney with care,
In hopes that St Nicholas soon would be there;
The children were nestled all snug in their beds,
While visions of sugarplums danced in their heads;

And Mamma in her 'kerchief, and I in my cap,
Had just settled our brains for a long winter's nap;
When out on the lawn there arose such a clatter
I sprang from the bed to see what was the matter.
Away to the window I flew like a flash,
Tore open the shutters and threw up the sash.

The moon, on the breast of the new-fallen snow,
Gave the lustre of midday to objects below,
When what to my wondering eyes should appear,
But a miniature sleigh, and eight tiny reindeer,
With a little old driver, so lively and quick,
I knew in a moment it must be St Nick.

More rapid than eagles his coursers they came,
And he whistled and shouted, and called them by name;
"Now, Dasher! Now, Dancer! Now, Prancer and Vixen!
On, Comet! On, Cupid! On, Donner and Blitzen!
To the top of the porch! To the top of the wall!
Now, dash away! Dash away! Dash away all!"

As dry leaves that before the wild hurricane fly,
When they meet with an obstacle, mount to the sky;
So up to the housetop the coursers they flew,
With the sleigh full of toys, and St Nicholas, too.

And then, in a twinkling, I heard on the roof
The prancing and pawing of each little hoof -
As I drew in my head, and was turning around,
Down the chimney St Nicholas came with a bound.

He was dressed all in fur, from his head to his foot,
And his clothes were all tarnished with ashes and soot;
A bundle of toys he had flung on his back,
And he looked like a pedlar just opening his pack.
His eyes - how they twinkled! His dimples, how merry!
His cheeks were like roses, his nose like a cherry!

His droll little mouth was drawn up like a bow,
And the beard of his chin was as white as the snow;
The stump of a pipe he held tight in his teeth,
And the smoke it encircled his head like a wreath;
He had a broad face and a little round belly
That shook, when he laughed, like a bowl full of jelly.

He was chubby and plump, a right jolly old elf,
And I laughed, when I saw him, in spite of myself;
A wink of his eye and a twist of his head,
Soon gave me to know I had nothing to dread;
He spoke not a word, but went straight to his work,
And filled all the stockings; then turned with a jerk,

And laying his finger aside of his nose,
And giving a nod, up the chimney he rose;
He sprang to his sleigh, to his team gave a whistle,
And away they all flew like the down of a thistle.
But I heard him exclaim, ere he drove out of sight,
"Happy Christmas to all, and to all a good night."

CHRISTMAS UNDERGROUND
from 'The Wind in the Willows' by Kenneth Grahame

"What a capital little house this is!" Mr Rat called out cheerily. "So compact! So well planned! Everything here and everything in its place! We'll make a jolly night of it. The first thing we want is a good fire; I'll see to that - I always know where to find things. So this is the parlour? Splendid! Your own idea, those little sleeping-bunks in the wall? Capital! Now, I'll fetch the wood and the coals, and you get a duster, Mole - you'll find one in the drawer of the kitchen table - and try and smarten things up a bit. Bustle about, old chap!"

Encouraged by his inspiring companion, the Mole roused himself and dusted and polished with energy and heartiness, while the Rat, running to and fro with armfuls of fuel, soon had a cheerful blaze roaring up the chimney. He hailed the Mole to come and warm himself; but Mole promptly had another fit of the blues, dropping down on a couch in dark despair and burying his face in his duster.

"Rat," he moaned, "how about your supper, you poor, cold, hungry, weary animal? I've nothing to give you - nothing - not a crumb!"

"What a fellow you are for giving in!" said the Rat reproachfully. "Why, only just now I saw a sardine-opener on the kitchen dresser, quite distinctly; and everybody knows that means there are sardines about somewhere in the neighbourhood. Rouse yourself! Pull yourself together, and come with me and forage."

They went and foraged accordingly, hunting through every cupboard and turning out every drawer. The result was not so very depressing after all, though of course it might have been better; a tin of sardines - a box of captain's biscuits, nearly full - and a German sausage encased in silver paper.

"There's a banquet for you!" observed the Rat, as he arranged the table. "I know some animals who would give their ears to be sitting down to supper with us tonight!"

"No bread!" groaned the Mole dolorously; "no butter, no - "

"No *pâté de foie gras*, no champagne!" continued the Rat, grinning. "And that reminds me - what's that little door at the end of the passage? Your cellar, of course! Every luxury in this house! Just you wait a minute."

He made for the cellar door, and presently reappeared, somewhat dusty, with a bottle of beer in each paw and another under each arm. "Self-indulgent beggar you seem to be, Mole," he observed. "Deny yourself nothing. This is really the jolliest little place I ever was in. Now, wherever did you pick up those prints? Make the place look so home-like, they do. No wonder you're so fond of it, Mole. Tell us all about it, and how you came to make it what it is."

Then, while the Rat busied himself fetching plates, and knives and forks, and mustard which he mixed in an egg-cup, the Mole, his bosom still heaving with the stress of his recent emotion, related - somewhat shyly at first, but with more freedom as he warmed to his subject - how this was planned, and how that was thought out, and how this was got through a windfall from an aunt, and that was a wonderful find and a bargain, and this other thing was bought out of laborious savings and a certain amount of 'going without'. His spirits finally quite restored, he must needs go and caress his possessions, and take a lamp and show off their points to his visitor, and expatiate on them, quite forgetful of the supper they both so much needed; Rat, who was desperately hungry but strove to conceal it, nodding seriously, examining with a puckered brow, and saying, "Wonderful", and "Most remarkable", at intervals, when the chance for an observation was given him.

At last the Rat succeeded in decoying him to the table, and had just got seriously to work with the sardine-opener when sounds were heard from the forecourt without - sounds like the scuffling of small feet in the gravel and a confused murmur of tiny voices, while broken sentences reached them - "Now, all in a line - hold the lantern up a bit, Tommy - clear your throats first - no coughing after I say one, two, three. - Where's young Bill? - Here, come on, do, we're all a-waiting - "

"What's up?" inquired the Rat, pausing in his labours.

"I think it must be the field-mice," replied the Mole, with a touch of pride in his manner. "They go round carol-singing regularly at this time of the year. They're quite an institution in these parts. And they never pass me over - they come to Mole End last of all; and I used to give them hot drinks, and supper sometimes, when I could afford it. It will be like old times to hear them again."

"Let's have a look at them!" cried the Rat, jumping up and running to the door.

It was a pretty sight, and a seasonable one, that met their eyes when they flung the door open. In the forecourt, lit by the dim rays of a horn lantern, some eight or ten little field-mice stood in a semi-circle, red worsted comforters round their throats, their forepaws thrust deep into their pockets, their feet jigging for warmth. With bright beady eyes they glanced shyly at each other, sniggering a little, sniffing and applying coatsleeves a good deal. As the door opened, one of the elder ones that carried the lantern was just saying, "Now then, one, two, three!" and forthwith their shrill little voices uprose on the air, singing one of the old-time carols that their forefathers composed in fields that were fallow and held by frost, or when snow-bound in chimney corners, and handed down to be sung in the miry street to lamp-lit windows at Yule-time.

> Villagers all, this frosty tide,
> Let your doors swing open wide,
> Though wind may follow, and snow beside,
> Yet draw us in by your fire to bide;
> > Joy shall be yours in the morning!

> Here we stand in the cold and the sleet,
> Blowing fingers and stamping feet,
> Come from far away you to greet -
> You by the fire and we in the street -
> > Bidding you joy in the morning!

> For ere one half of the night was gone,
> Sudden a star has led us on,
> Raining bliss and benison -
> Bliss tomorrow and more anon,
> > Joy for every morning!

Goodman Joseph toiled through the snow-
Saw the star o'er a stable low;
Mary she might not further go -
Welcome thatch, and litter below!
        Joy was hers in the morning!

And when they heard the angels tell
'Who were the first to cry Nowell?
Animals all, as it befell,
In the stable where they did dwell!
        Joy shall be theirs in the morning!'

The voices ceased, the singers, bashful but smiling, exchanged sidelong glances, and silence succeeded - but for a moment only. Then, from up above and far away, down the tunnel they had so lately travelled was borne to their ears in a faint musical hum the sound of distant bells ringing a joyful and clangorous peal.

"Very well sung, boys!" cried the Rat heartily. "And now come along in, all of you, and warm yourselves by the fire, and have something hot!"

"Yes, come along, field-mice," cried the Mole eagerly. "This is quite like old times! Shut the door after you. Pull up that settle to the fire. Now, you just wait a minute, while we - O, Ratty!" he cried in despair, plumping down on a seat, with tears impending. "Whatever are we doing? We've nothing to give them!"

"You leave all that to me," said the masterful Rat. "Here, you with the lantern! Come over this way. I want to talk to you. Now, tell me, are there any shops open at this hour of the night?"

"Why, certainly, sir," replied the field-mouse respectfully. "At this time of the year our shops keep open to all sorts of hours."

"Then look here!" said the Rat. "You go off at once, you and your lantern, and you get me - "

Here much muttered conversation ensued, and the Mole only heard bits of it, such as - "Fresh, mind! - no, a pound of that will do - see you get Buggins's, for I won't have any other - no, only the best - if you can't get it there, try somewhere else - yes, of course, home-made, no tinned stuff - well then, do the best you can!" Finally, there was a chink of coin passing from paw to paw, the field-mouse was provided with an ample basket for his purchases, and off he hurried, he and his lantern.

The rest of the field-mice, perched in a row on the settle, their small legs swinging, gave themselves up to the enjoyment of the fire, and toasted their chilblains till they tingled; while the Mole, failing to draw them into easy conversation, plunged into family history and made each of them recite the names of his numerous brothers, who were too young, it appeared, to be allowed to go out a-carolling this year, but looked forward very shortly to winning the parental consent.

BABOUSCKA (Also known as 'Baboushka')
by Carolyn Sherwin Bailey

It was the night the dear Christ Child came to Bethlehem. In a country far away from Him, an old woman named Babouscka sat in her snug little house by her warm fire. The wind was drifting the snow outside and howling down the chimney, but it only made Babouscka's fire burn more brightly.

"How glad I am that I may stay indoors!" said Babouscka, holding her hands out to the bright blaze.

But suddenly she heard a loud rap at her door. She opened it and her candle shone on three old men standing outside in the snow. Their beards were as white as the snow, and so long that they reached the ground. Their eyes shone kindly in the light of Babouscka's candle, and their arms were full of precious things - boxes of jewels, and sweet-smelling oils, and ointments.

"We have travelled far, Babouscka," they said, "and we stop to tell you of the Baby Prince born this night in Bethlehem. He comes to rule the world and teach all men to be loving and true. We carry Him gifts. Come with us, Babouscka!"

But Babouscka looked at the driving snow, and then inside at her cosy room and the crackling fire.

"It is too late to go with you, good sirs," she said. "The weather is too cold."

She went inside again and shut the door, and the old men journeyed on to Bethlehem without her. But as Babouscka sat by her fire, rocking, she began to think about the little Christ Child, for she loved all babies.

"Tomorrow I will go to find Him," she said - "tomorrow, when it is light. And I will carry Him some toys."

So when it was morning Babouscka put on her long cloak, and took her staff, and filled her basket with the pretty things a baby would like - gold balls, and wooden toys, and strings of silver cobwebs - and she set out to find the Christ Child.

But, oh! Babouscka had forgotten to ask the three old men the road to Bethlehem, and they had travelled so far through the night that she could not overtake them. Up and down the roads she hurried, through woods and fields and towns, saying to whomsoever she met:

"I go to find the Christ Child. Where does He lie? I bring some pretty toys for His sake." But no one could tell her the way to go, and they all said, "Farther on, Babouscka, farther on."

So she travelled on, and on, and on for years and years - but she never found the little Christ Child.

They say that old Babouscka is travelling still, looking for Him. When it comes to Christmas Eve, and the children are lying fast asleep, Babouscka comes softly through the snowy fields and towns, wrapped in her long cloak and carrying her basket on her arm. With her staff she raps gently at the doors and goes inside and holds her candle close to the children's faces.

"Is He here?" she asks. "Is the little Christ Child here?" And then she turns sorrowfully away again, crying, "Farther on, farther on." But before she leaves, she takes a toy from her basket and lays it beside the pillow for a Christmas gift. "For His sake," she says softly, and then hurries on through the years and forever in search of the little Christ Child.

A Humorous Christmas

THE VISITATION
by Gervase Phinn

One December, I was invited to a Nativity play held in a school in one of the few industrial towns in my area. Joseph, a rather fat boy dressed in a Mexican poncho and a towel over his head, did not look entirely happy when he heard the news of the imminent arrival of the baby.

"Are you sure about this?" he asked, an anxious expression suffusing his round face.

"Course I'm sure!" Mary replied. "An Angel of the Lord told me."

"Are you sure it was an angel?"

"Course I'm sure. Her name was Gabrielle."

Hearing this, I remembered that the school was very big on equal opportunities.

"I think I'm going to faint," Joseph sighed.

"Pull yourself together. It's great news. Angel Gabrielle told me not to be frightened."

"I'm dead worried about this, Mary," Joseph confided, shaking his head solemnly "It's come as a big shock."

"There's nothing to worry about, silly. Everything will be all right."

71

"I suppose we'll have to get married then."

"S'pose so."

"Are you sure you're having a baby, Mary?" Joseph persisted.

"Yes, I've told you, and we're going to call Him Jesus and He will be the best baby in the whole wide world and we will love Him very, very much and take care of Him."

Joseph nodded but still didn't look too happy. "All right then," he sighed.

How many young couples, I thought to myself that afternoon as I watched the small children act out their play, had been in that situation?

At one little primary school, deep in the Dales, I attended an unforgettable Nativity play which was improvised by the children. This is not always a good idea because small children can be very unpredictable, particularly when faced with an appreciative audience.

Mary, a pretty little thing of about six or seven, was busy bustling about the stage, wiping and dusting, when the Angel of the Lord appeared stage right. The heavenly spirit was a tall, self-conscious boy with a plain, pale face and sticky-out ears. He was dressed in a flowing white robe, large paper wings and sported a tinsel halo, somewhat crooked. Having wiped his nose on his sleeve, he glanced around suspiciously then sidled up to Mary, as a dodgy market-trader might, to see if you were interested in buying something from 'under the counter'.

"Who are you?" Mary asked sharply, putting down her duster and placing her hands on her hips. This was not the quietly spoken, gentle-natured Mary I was used to.

"I'm the Angel Gabriel," the boy replied with a deadpan expression and in a flat voice.

"Well, what do you want?"

"Are you Mary?"

"Yes."

"I come with tidings of great joy."

"What?"

"I've got some good news."

"What is it?"

"You're having a baby."

"I'm not."

"You are."

"Who says?"

"God, and He sent me to tell you."

"Well, I don't know nothing about this."

"And it will be a boy and He will become great and be called - er, um ... - " The boy stalled for a moment. Ah - called Son of the Most High, the King of Kings. He will rule for ever and His reign will have no end."

"What if it's a girl?"

"It won't be."

"You don't know. It might be."

"It won't, 'cos God knows about these things."

"Oh."

"And you must call it Jesus."

"I don't like the name Jesus. Can I call Him something else?"

"No."

"What about Gavin?"

"No!" the angel snapped.

"You have to call it Jesus. Otherwise you don't get it."

"All right then," Mary agreed.

"And look after it."

"I don't know what I'm going to tell Joseph," the little girl said, putting on a worried expression and picking up her duster.

"Tell him it's God's."

"OK," Mary said, smiling for the first time.

When the Angel of the Lord had departed Joseph entered. He was a cheeky-faced little boy dressed in a brown woollen dressing gown, thick blue socks and a multicoloured towel over his head, held in place by the inevitable elastic belt with a snake clasp.

"Hello, Mary," he said cheerfully.

"Oh hello, Joseph," Mary replied.

"Have you had a good day?"

"Yes, pretty good really," she told him, nodding theatrically

"Have you anything to tell me?"

There was a slight pause before she replied. "I am having a baby - oh, and it's not yours."

NO ROOM AT THE INN
by Gervase Phinn

Mums and dads, grannies and grandpas, aunties and uncles, neighbours and friends filled the school hall for the Nativity play, the highlight of the school year. I found a seat just as the lights dimmed and a spotlight lit up the small stage.

The curtain opened to reveal the outlines of various eastern-looking houses painted on a backdrop and two rather forlorn palm trees made out of papier mâché and green crêpe paper which drooped in the centre of the stage.

The little boy playing the lead as Joseph entered wearing a brightly coloured towel over his head. He took centre stage without a trace of nerves, stared at the audience and then beckoned a particularly worried-looking Mary who entered, pulling behind her a large cardboard-and-polystyrene donkey.

"Come on!" urged Joseph. "Hurry up!" He banged on the door of one of the houses. "Open up! Open up!" he shouted loudly.

The Innkeeper, with a face like a death mask, threw open the door. "What?" he barked.

"Have you any room?"

"No!"

"You have!"

"I haven't!"

"You have, I saw t'light on."

"I haven't."

"Look, we've travelled all t'night, up and down those sand-dunes, through dusty towns, over hills, in and out of rivers. We're fit to drop."

"Can't help that, there's no room," replied the Innkeeper.

"And I've got t'wife out here on t'donkey." Joseph gestured in the direction of a very glum-looking Mary who was staring at the audience, completely motionless.

The Innkeeper remained unmoved. "And you can't leave that donkey there. You'll have to move it!"

"Well, give us a room."

"There is no room in the inn. How many more times do I have to tell you?"

"She's having a babby, tha knaws."

"Well, I can't help that, it's nowt to do with me."

"I know," replied Joseph sighing as he turned to the audience, "and its nowt to do with me neither."

To the surprise of the children there were great guffaws of laughter from the audience.

And so the play progressed until the final magic moment. Little rosy-faced angels in white with cardboard wings and tinsel haloes, shepherds with towels over their heads and cotton-wool beards, the Three Kings in coloured robes and shiny paper hats gathered around Mary and Joseph on the cramped stage to sing 'Away in a Manger' and bring a tear to every eye.

YOU CAN'T COVER UP A SHINY NOSE
by Oliver Pritchett

This is one of the most exciting publishing events of the decade. We are immensely proud to announce that this column has acquired the serial rights to the autobiography of the distinguished reindeer, Rudolph. This book is bound to cause a sensation, as Rudolph makes many outspoken comments about some of his colleagues pulling Santa's sleigh.

I have never allowed my shiny nose to stop me leading a full life. Although I had to put up with some sneering in the early days, I believe I proved my worth on that notorious foggy Christmas Eve when Santa called on me and my nose to light his sleigh. It is a source of great pride to me that I did not let him down on that occasion.

After that, I received a good deal of favourable reaction from most of the media. *The Sun* was kind enough to run a headline saying: '*The Sun shouts it out with glee: Rudolph the Red-Nosed Reindeer, you'll go down in historee*'.

Perhaps having a shiny nose has made me too frank at times. I have to be honest about my nose; I can't cover it up or powder it. Maybe this makes me too honest for comfort. It's also true that my integrity shines as brightly as my nose. You would even say it glows. And so it lights up some of the darker corners of this sleigh-pulling business.

It has been said that I am arrogant and perhaps that is true. It's hard not to be arrogant when you've had a popular song written about you which is heard in shops throughout the land at this time of year.

Santa constantly tells us reindeer that we must all pull together and that we must show unity so that we come out looking good on the Christmas cards. However we are all individuals.

Dasher and Dancer are ultra-loyal Claus-ites, but they are weak. They tend to panic on rooftops. In the Christmas of 2001 Dancer went absolutely to pieces on a roof somewhere near Newcastle that was a bit steeper and more slippery than normal. He kept yelping: 'We're going to fall off! We're doomed!' Fortunately the media never found out. Donner is a bit of a bully and throws his weight about. He likes to jingle the harness to assert himself. Once he saw that I would stand up to him and not be intimidated, he came to respect me as a colleague.

Blitzen is all antlers and no sense. Quite honestly, I don't know what he's doing in the front rank of a reindeer team when he'd be more suited to nosing about in the snow for moss in one of the less demanding regions of Lapland.

As for the others, Vixen has no strategic sense at all, Comet has gone soft and taken his hoof off the accelerator and Cupid is several flakes short of a snowman. As for Prancer, when I moved into his stall in the reindeer stable at Santa's headquarters, I found he had left it in a total mess. He likes to go his own way, which is no help when you are pulling a heavy sleigh and having to meet some tough delivery targets.

I'd be the first to admit that Santa has a difficult job and, on the whole, he does it pretty well. He is incredibly sensitive about his nickname, 'Three Hos', and doesn't like it at all when the media mention it. And he can't disguise his irritation when people make jokes about his waistline and wonder how he manages to fit into chimneys. He gets into a real fury when the elves tease him and chant, like football crowds, 'Who ate all the mince pies?'

Basically, he's insecure. He's desperate for people to keep on believing in him, so he spends too much time putting in personal appearances in stores and Christmas fairs. He makes us reindeer haul the sleigh up to ridiculous heights, flying in front of the moon in silhouette, just to get some good footage on the 10 o'clock television news. Santa's tragedy is that, actually, these days more people believe in me than in him.

WILLIAM JOINS THE WAITS
from 'Just William at Christmas' by Richmal Crompton

William met Ginger and Douglas the next morning.

"I'm goin' waitin' (Carol Singing) Christmas Eve," he announced proudly.

"So'm I," said Ginger.

"So'm I," said Douglas.

It turned out that Mr Solomon had visited their parents too, yesterday, and to their parents, too, had expressed doubt as to the advisability of their sons being allowed to join the party. Though well meaning, he was not a very tactful young man, and had not expressed his doubts in such a way as to placate maternal pride.

"My mother said," said Ginger, "why shun't I go same as anyone else, so I'm goin'!"

"So did mine," said Douglas, "so so'm I."

"Yes," said William indignantly, "fancy sayin' he thought I'd better not come. Why, I should think I'm 's good at waitin' 's anybody else in the world - why, when I start singin' you c'n hear me at the other end of the village."

This statement, being unassailable, passed unchallenged.

"Do you know where we're goin'?" continued William.

"He said beginnin' up Well Lane," said Douglas.

"My Uncle George lives in Well Lane," said Ginger thoughtfully, "the one what's givin' me *Kings an' Queens of England*."

There was a short silence. In that silence the thought came to all three Outlaws that the expedition might have even vaster possibilities than at first they had imagined.

"*Then*, where we goin'?" said William.

"Jus' up the village street," said Douglas.

"My Uncle Charles," said William thoughtfully, "the one what's givin' me the penknife you can't do any harm with, lives right away from the village."

"So does my Aunt Jane - the one what's givin' me the ole green tie." William's face assumed its expression of daring leadership.

"Well," he said, "we'll jus' have to do what we can."

Many, many times before Christmas Eve arrived did Mr Solomon bitterly regret the impulse on which he had suggested his party of waits. He would have liked to cancel the arrangement altogether, but he lacked the courage.

He held several practices in which his party of full-voiced but unmelodious musicians roared 'Good King Wenceslas' and 'The First Noël', making up in volume for what they lacked in tone and technique. During these practices he watched the Outlaws apprehensively. His apprehensions increased as time went on, for the Outlaws were behaving like creatures from another and a higher world.

They were docile and obedient and respectful. And this was not normal in the Outlaws. Normally they would by now have tired of the whole thing. Normally they would be clustered in the back row cracking nuts and throwing the shells at friends or foes. But they were not. They were standing in the front row wearing saintly expressions (as far, that is, as the expressions of the Outlaws could convey the idea of saintliness), singing 'Good King Wenceslas Looked Out' with strident conscientiousness.

Mr Solomon would have been relieved to see them cracking nuts or deliberately introducing discords into the melody (they introduced discords, it is true, but unconsciously). He began to have a horrible suspicion that they were forming some secret plan.

The prospective waits assembled with Mr Solomon at the end of the village at nightfall. Mr Solomon was intensely nervous. It had taken all his better self to resist the temptation to put the whole thing off on the fictitious excuse of sudden illness. He held a lantern in his hand and a large tin of sweets under his arm. He had bought the large tin of sweets last night on the spur of the moment. He had a vague hope that it might prove useful in some crisis.

He raised the lantern and examined the little crowd of faces around him. He looked as though he were counting them. In reality he was anxiously ascertaining whether the Outlaws were there. He'd been clinging all day to the hope that the Outlaws mightn't be there. After all, he had thought hopefully, there was quite a lot of measles about. Or they might have forgotten. But his heart sank. There they were, standing in the very centre of the group. He sighed. Probably there were hundreds of boys all over the world coming out in rashes at that moment, and yet here were these boys as bloomingly healthy as they'd ever been. Life was full of irony.

"Well, here we are," he said in that voice of rather painful brightness that he always used with the young. "Here we all are ... All got your best voices, eh? Now we'll go down Well Lane first."

"Uncle George," whispered Ginger.

"Go straight down the lane," said Mr Solomon, "till you get to the Laurels, and then turn in and we'll begin with 'The First Noël'. "

Obediently the little troupe set off towards Well Lane. It was as quiet and good and orderly as a Sunday School superintendent's heart could wish, and yet the Sunday School superintendent's heart was not quite light. He could not help remembering the proverbial order of sequence of the calm and the storm.

He'd have felt, of course, quite happy if the Outlaws hadn't been there.

He had, however, taken quite a lot of trouble over the itinerary. He meant only to pay half-a-dozen visits, and to sing only one carol at each. It was not likely that they would receive any encores. The whole thing ought to be over in an hour. He hoped it would be, anyway.

He had already prepared the householders who were to be

honoured by a visit from his waits, and though not enthusiastic they were ready to receive the visitants in a Christmas spirit of good will. He meant to risk no unchristian reception by paying unexpected visits. Though he was well-meaning rather than musical still he had a vague suspicion that the performance of his choir left a good deal to be desired.

The Misses Perkins lived at the Laurels, and they had assured Mr Solomon that they would love - simply *love* - to hear the dear little boys sing Christmas carols, and so would Muffy. (Muffy was the Misses Perkins' cat.) The visit to the Misses Perkins, anyway, ought to go off nicely. Fortunately, the Misses Perkins were slightly deaf.

Everything seemed to be going off very nicely so far. The waits were walking quietly and sedately down the road, not shouting or fighting as boys so often did. Mr Solomon's spirits rose. It was really after all a very beautiful idea - and they were really after all very nice boys. He could see William and Ginger and Douglas walking decorously and silently together. Marvellous how even such boys as those yielded to the Christmas spirit. They were walking at the head, leading the little troupe; they were turning obediently in at the gate of the Laurels. The young man took out his tuning fork and followed, smiling proudly.

Then the light of his lantern shone upon the gate as he entered and - it wasn't the Laurels.

They'd made a mistake. It wasn't the Laurels. It was the Cedars. Mr Solomon, of course, could not know that the Outlaws had passed the Laurels and entered the Cedars deliberately because Ginger's Uncle George lived at the Cedars.

"Come back!" called Mr Solomon's thin voice through the night. "It's the wrong house! Come back!"

But already the waits had burst violently into 'The First Noël'. It was a pity that they did not wait for the note from Mr Solomon, who had his tuning fork already in his hand.

It was a pity that they did not begin all together, and that having begun each at a separate moment each should cling so tenaciously to his own time and interpretation. It was a great pity that they did not know the words.

It was the greatest pity of all that they possessed the voices they did possess. But there is no denying their zest. There is no denying that each one put all the power and energy he possessed into his rendering of the carol. The resulting sound was diabolical. Diabolical is a strong word, but it is hardly strong enough. The English language does not really possess a word strong enough to describe the effect of these waits' rendering of 'The First Noël'.

After one minute of it, Uncle George's window was flung up and Uncle George's purple face was thrust out.

"Go away, you young devils!" he sputtered. "How *dare* you come here kicking up that infernal din? Go a-*way*, I say!"

Mr Solomon's voice in the rear kept up its shrill but ineffective plaint. "Come away, boys - it's the wrong house. I said the Laurels - the Misses Perkins and Muffy will be wondering wherever we are - quietly, boys - don't shout so - and you've got the wrong note - "

But nobody heard him. The uproar continued to be deafening. The other waits realised that the Outlaws were for some reason or other determined to make as much noise as possible and gladly gave their assistance. They found the process exhilarating. They began to think that the whole affair was going to be more interesting than they had thought it would be. Joyfully they yelled and yelled and yelled. Above them the purple-faced figure of Uncle George gesticulated and uttered words which were (fortunately, perhaps) drowned by the inferno of sound below.

Then, suddenly, silence came. Abruptly the Outlaws had stopped singing and the others at once stopped too, waiting developments. It was, of course, Uncle George's chance, and the immediate development was a flood of eloquence from Uncle George, to which the waits listened with joyful interest and at which Mr Solomon grew pale.

"Pardon me, sir," gasped Mr Solomon, at last recovering. "Quite a mistake - boys mistook house - visit meant for friends of ours - no offence intended, I assure you."

But so breathless was he that only the two boys nearest him heard him, and no one heeded him. For to the amazement of all of them (except Ginger and Douglas), William spoke up firmly from the foreground.

"Please, sir, we're c'lectin' books for our library. Please sir, can you give us a book for our lib'ry?"

Mr Solomon gaped in open-mouthed amazement at this statement. He tried to utter some protest, but could only stutter.

Uncle George, however, could do more than stutter. He answered the question in the negative with such strength, and at such length, that the waits' admiration of him became a sort of ecstasy. William answered the refusal by bursting with amazing promptitude and discord into 'Good King Wenceslas'.

The Outlaws followed his lead. The rest of the waits joined in, most of them showing their conservative spirits by clinging still to 'The First Noël'. Not that it mattered much. No listener could have told what any of them was singing. Words and tune were lost in a tornado of unmelodious sound. Each wait tasted the rapture of exerting the utmost force of his lungs, and trying to drown his neighbour's effort.

In front of them Uncle George hung out of his bedroom window gesticulating violently, his complexion changing from purple to black.

Behind them Mr Solomon clung to the gatepost of the Cedars, moaning softly and mopping his brow.

A second time the waits stopped suddenly at a signal from William. The nightmare sound died away and there followed a silence broken only by the moans of Mr Solomon and sputtering from Uncle George, in which could be recognised the oft-returning words 'the police'.

But something of Uncle George's first fine careless frenzy was gone. There was something broken about him, as there would indeed have been something broken about anyone who had listened to the ghastly sound. Again William spoke up brightly.

"Please c'n you give us a book for our lib'ry? We're collectin' books for our lib'ry. We want a book for boys - 'bout history, please. If you've got one to give us. For our lib'ry please."

In the background, Mr Solomon, still clinging to the gatepost, moaned. "I assure you, sir - mistake - wrong house - "

With admirable promptness and a force that was amazing considering the energy that he must have already expended, William burst with sudden unexpected violence into 'Fight the Good Fight', which Mr Solomon had been teaching them the Sunday before. It was taken up by the others, each, as before, striking out an entirely independent line in his rendering of it. It was the last straw. Uncle George was beaten.

With an expression of agony he clapped his hands over his ears and staggered backwards. Then he reappeared, and *The Kings and Queens of*

England hit William a smart blow on the side of his head, and fell on to the gravel at his feet. William picked it up and signalled that the hymn should cease. A moment later the waits had gone. There only remained Mr Solomon clinging to the gatepost, stupefied by the terrible events he had just lived through, and Uncle George sputtering at the open window.

Uncle George's sputtering suddenly ceased, and he hurled at Mr Solomon's figure, dimly perceived through the darkness, a flood of eloquence which was worthy of a more discerning and appreciative audience.

Mr Solomon looked around him wildly. He looked for his lantern. It was gone. He looked for his tin of sweets. It was gone. He looked for his waits. They were gone.

Pursued by Uncle George's lurid invective he fled into the road and looked up and down it. There was no sign of lantern or tin of sweets or waits. He tore along to the village street where he had told them to go next and where presumably their next warned host awaited them.

There was no sign of them.

Distracted he tore up and down the road.

Then at the end of the road there appeared the tall burly figure of - a policeman. Unstrung by his experience, the blameless Mr Solomon fled from the minion of the law like a criminal and ran as fast as his legs could carry him homewards.

MY TWELVE DAYS OF CHRISTMAS
Anonymous

On the first day of Christmas, my true love said to me,
"I'm glad we bought fresh turkey and a proper Christmas tree."

On the second day of Christmas, much laughter could be heard,
As we tucked into our turkey, a most delicious bird.

On the third day we entertained the people from next door.
The turkey tasted just as good as it had the day before.

Day four, relations came to stay, poor Gran is looking old.
We finished up the Christmas pud and ate the turkey cold.

On the fifth day of Christmas, outside the snowflakes flurried,
But we were nice and warm inside, and we had our turkey curried.

On the sixth day, I must admit, the Christmas spirit died,
The children fought and bickered, we ate turkey rissoles, fried.

On the seventh day of Christmas, I saw my true love wince,
When he sat down at the table and was offered turkey mince.

Day eight, and nerves were getting frayed, the dog had run for shelter.
I served up turkey pancakes, then we needed Alka Seltzer.

On the ninth day of Christmas, by lunchtime Dad was blotto,
But said it helped him face a lunch of turkey rice risotto.

By the tenth day the booze had gone (except our home-made brew).
And if that wasn't bad enough we suffered turkey stew.

On the eleventh day of Christmas, the Christmas tree was moulting.
The mince pies were hard as rock and the turkey quite revolting.

But on the twelfth day, my true love had a smile upon his lips,
The guests had gone, the turkey too, and we dined on fish and chips.

The True Meaning of Christmas

CALL ME BLESSED

by Jacqueline Wilson
Adapted from the original

When will it be over? She had no idea it would hurt so much. She wants her Mother. She wants Elizabeth. She wants her womenfolk. She had it all planned. It was going to be so beautiful. She was going to stay calm and in control. She wasn't going to cry. She'd lie on her soft bedding in her clean little house and look at the sky through the slit of the window. She'd look up to her Lord and she'd pray to him through every pain.

She tries to pray now but the pain keeps flashing through her like lightning and she can't think properly. Her whispers become gasps, cries, screams. She calls to the Lord because she is his chosen maiden but she can't find him. It's dark and there's just the thunder of her cries and the lightning of her pain.

Oh why couldn't this have waited till she was back home? Home in her house, on her soft cushions, with her womenfolk to hold her hands and sponge her face and stroke her poor swollen body. Everything is ready for this at home. There is the little cradle of twigs, the clean linen, the sweet smelling ointments. Why is it so impatient? Why choose this filthy cave at the back of a stranger's house? The only bed is the straw, the only linen the veil from her head. Why does it want to be born in this dark and lonely place reeking of animal dung?

The cattle munch and murmur, oblivious, but her own little donkey lifts its head and brays uneasily as if it's in pain too. It's lame after the long journey. Oh that endless trek through Samaria, the sharp bones of the little ass chafing her thighs, the dust coating her skin, lining her garments, the tension turning every muscle into a sharp stone. She got so unbearably stiff that she slid down from the donkey and tried to walk but she couldn't cope with the clumsiness of her body. She wanted to run like the wind but she could only shamble like a beggar. She had to be helped back on to the little ass, weak and sweating, the pains already flickering in her stomach and spine.

She didn't dare acknowledge them. She stayed silent all that last dusty day. She bent her head so that the pain wouldn't show on her face. She knew it was too soon, she knew she'd have no-one to help her, she knew it was a nightmare when she so wanted it to be like a golden dream. Like her golden dream of Gabriel. The golden voice, the golden heat, the brush of golden wings and then the golden trumpets inside her head proclaiming her awesome gift from God.

Sometimes the trumpets were not quite loud enough. She could hear Joseph's words, she could see his anguish and shame. Some said he should spurn her, some even said he should stone her! But he stood up with her in front of all the villagers and he married her, even though he knew she was carrying a child that wasn't his.

"A golden child. God's only son. He chose me Joseph. An angel came down from Heaven and seared me with the golden spirit and now I have God's golden child within me", she whispered on their wedding night, going down on her knees to Joseph to make him understand. But he couldn't hear the trumpets even though her head rang with their golden harmonies. He turned away from her.

"Joseph, for pity's sake, come to me!" She calls again and again. She calls until her voice is hoarse. And then she hears a rustle in the straw, senses a large shape above her and smells the faint scent of sycamore clinging to his clothing. He crouches beside her. There's a lull between the lightning and she struggles to sit up, to see his face in the murk of the moonlight. She sees the salt glitter on his cheeks.

"Don't hate me husband", she gasps.

"I don't hate you Mary. I've tried to hate you but I love you too much. I've loved you since you were a small girl skipping past my shop. Remember, I pinned a few wood-shavings in your hair for fancy curls. You looked so shy and solemn at first but then you saw your shadow in the sunlight and you smiled at your silly curls. That smile stirred strong feelings in my heart. I knew then that all I wanted in the whole world was to make you my wife. I am your husband now but I am helpless. I don't know what to do for you. I can't bear to see you struggling like this."

"Stay with me. Please stay with me."

The lightning strikes and she screams and flails her arms and he catches hold of her, gripping with his strong hands until the thunder stops crashing.

"I'll stay with you," Joseph whispers into the darkness. "You are my wife and I am your husband. I will stay."

She has lived as a maiden since her marriage but now the storm in her body blows away all her modesty. She forgets that she is Mary. She is part of the storm, the bellow of thunder, the flash of lightning, and she rages. She is torn one way, torn another, torn until she is suddenly, shockingly split into two. Two people. She is one and he is the other. Still joined but separate. The storm is over.

She reaches down and holds him in her hands. She stares at him in wonder. She stares at the bloom of his cheeks, pink as pomegranates. She stares at the milky paleness of his tiny wrists, the spiderweb delicacy of his veins. She lays him on her head-dress but before she swaddles him she wants to worship him. She rubs her cheek against the damp tendrils of his hair. She kisses one tiny curled foot. She touches one small clenching fist and it fastens round her finger. There is no doubt now. He is her golden gift from God.

She wraps him up reverently, her hands trembling. She holds him in her arms and shudders as one more lightning flicker contracts her womb. In that searing second she sees herself still holding him in her arms when he's a grown man. A golden grown man and yet he seems as stiff and still as a babe in swaddling clothes. Tears stream from her eyes although she doesn't understand why.

"Don't cry, my dearest wife", Joseph whispers, and he kisses her eyes. "The pain is all over now."

But she knows it is only just beginning.

THE OXEN
by Thomas Hardy

Christmas Eve, and twelve of the clock.
"Now they are all on their knees,"
An elder said as we sat in a flock
By the embers in hearthside ease.

We pictured the meek mild creatures where
They dwelt in their strawy pen,
Nor did it occur to one of us there
To doubt they were kneeling then.

So fair a fancy few would weave
In these years! Yet, I feel,
If someone said on Christmas Eve,
"Come; see the oxen kneel

In the lonely barton by yonder coomb
Our childhood used to know,"
I should go with him in the gloom,
Hoping it might be so.

THE MARCH OF THE THREE KINGS
by Ursula Vaughan Williams (b 1911)

From kingdoms of wisdom secret and far
come Caspar, Melchior, Balthasar;
they ride through time, they ride through night,
led by the star's foretelling light.

Crowning the skies
the star of morning, star of dayspring calls,
lighting the stable and the broken walls
where the prince lies.

Gold from the veins of earth he brings,
red gold to crown the King of Kings.
Power and glory here behold
shut in a talisman of gold.

Frankincense from those dark hands
was gathered in eastern, sunrise lands,
incense to burn both night and day
to bear the prayers a priest will say.

Myrrh is a bitter gift for the dead.
Birth but begins the path you tread;
your way is short, your days foretold
by myrrh and frankincense and gold.

Return to kingdoms secret and far,
Caspar, Melchior, Balthasar,
ride through the desert, retrace the night
leaving the star's imperial light

Crowning the skies
the star of morning, star of dayspring, calls:
clear on the hilltop its sharp radiance falls
lighting the stable and the broken walls
where the prince lies.

JOURNEY OF THE MAGI
by T S Eliot

"A cold coming we had of it,
Just the worst time of the year
For a journey, and such a long journey;
The ways deep and the weather sharp,
The very dead of winter."
And the camels galled, sore-footed, refractory,
Lying down in the melting snow.
There were times we regretted
The summer palaces on slopes, the terraces,
And the silken girls bringing sherbet.
Then the camel men cursing and grumbling
And running away, and wanting their liquor and women,
And the night-fires going out, and the lack of shelters,
And the cities hostile and the towns unfriendly
And the villages dirty and charging high prices:
A hard time we had of it.
At the end we preferred to travel all night,
Sleeping in snatches,
With the voices singing in our ears, saying
That this was all folly.

Then at dawn we came down to a temperate valley,
Wet, below the snow line, smelling of vegetation,
With a running stream and a water-mill beating the darkness,
And three trees on the low sky.
And an old white horse galloped away in the meadow.
Then we came to a tavern with vine-leaves over the lintel,
Six hands at an open door dicing for pieces of silver,
And feet kicking the empty wine-skins.
But there was no information, so we continued
And arrived at evening, not a moment too soon
Finding the place; it was (you may say) satisfactory.

All this was a long time ago, I remember,
And I would do it again, but set down
This set down
This: were we led all that way for
Birth or Death? There was a Birth, certainly,
We had evidence and no doubt. I had seen birth and death,
But had thought they were different; this Birth was
Hard and bitter agony for us, like Death, our death.
We returned to our places, these Kingdoms,
But no longer at ease here, in the old dispensation,
With an alien people clutching their gods.
I should be glad of another death.

Closing
Sentiments

A YORKSHIRE NATIVITY
from 'A Wayne in a Manger' by Gervase Phinn

With each season this vast, beautiful Yorkshire landscape changes dramatically but it is in winter that the most spectacular transformation takes place. It is then that the multicoloured canvas of pale green fields and dark fells, twisting roads and endless silvered walls, clustered farmsteads and stone cottages, squat churches and ancient inns is enveloped in one endless white covering, and a strange, colourless world stroked by silence emerges.

It was on a bright, cold morning, a week before the schools broke up for the Christmas holidays, that I went to Staplemoor Primary School and met William again. The last time I had visited the school it had been on a mild autumn afternoon. Gone now were the brilliant autumnal colours, the golden lustre of the trees, the thick carpet of yellow and orange leaves and the rusty bracken slopes. Now it was a patchwork of white, criss-crossed with the stone walls. The scene was magical.

I had met William, a round-faced boy of about ten or eleven, with apple-red cheeks, a thatch of black hair and a ready smile, on the previous occasion and remembered him as a very likeable and forthcoming young lad.

He now presented himself to me with a broad grin. "Mester Phinn, in't it?" he said.

"That's right," I replied.

"Schoil hinspector."

"You remember me?"

"Oh, aye. Once met, never forgotten. I've a good memory for faces. How's tha doin' ?"

"I'm fine, thank you, and what about you?"

"Champion," he replied.

"And looking forward to Christmas?"

"Aye, cooarse I am. Best time o' year is Christmas."

"And what do you like best about Christmas?" I asked.

The boy sucked in his lips and folded his arms. "There's summat special abaat it, in't there?" he said. "People smile more, they look 'appier. All t'shops are colourful and bright. I can't think what I likes the best. I love it in t'kitchen watchin' mi mam start baking 'er puddings and cakes an' mince pies an' I can sit in front o' fire scraping t'bowl out afterwards. I like it when me an' mi dad go up to Durdeyfield Farm to get a gret big fir tree an' we purr it up an' me an' mi sister decorate it. Then t'turkey and t'goose arrive ready for pluckin'. That's my job, that. And if it snows, we all gu sledgin' down Ribbon Bank. Then on Boxin' Day, we watch 'unters and 'ounds 'ammering along 'igh street goin' to t'meet. Aye, it's a grand time o' year is Christmas."

"I remember thinking the last time we met, William, what a bright and confident lad you were," I told him.

"Aye, well, I think I told thee then, Mester Phinn, that mi granddad says not to be backwards in comin' for'ards. 'Allus speak tha mind. Say what tha's got to say an' then shurrup.' That's what he says."

"Wise words," I said.

"Come Christmas mornin', we'll all be 'earin' 'im preachin' at t'chapel in t'village. I think I towld thee 'e's a Methodist lay preacher last time tha were 'ere. I reckon 'e's every bit as good as what John Wesley was. I love to 'ear mi granddad tellin' t'Christmas story. 'E allus tells it in 'is own way, Yorkshire fashion."

"I've never heard the Christmas story told in the Yorkshire fashion," I said. "Perhaps you would like to tell me."

"Ay, all reight," he replied. "I've 'eard it offen enough but it's worth repeatin'. " Then, coughing dramatically, the boy began.

"It were reight cowld that neet when Mary an' Joseph arrived at t'inn. "No room!" said t'Innkeeper. "Thas'll aff to gu raand back in t'barn 'cos we're full to bustin', what wi' all fowk comin' to pay their taxes. It's not too bad in t'barn, it's warm and dry an' out of t'cowld an' I'll fetch thee a couple o' blankets round when tha's settled in." So Mary and Joseph went round t'back an into t'barn an med best on it. Meanwhile, in t'fields nearby were these shepherds watching ovver t'sheep. All on a sudden, a reight bright light shines down on 'em. "Hey up," says one of t'shepherds, "what's to do?" Theer stood this hangel, wi' wings o' fire an' an 'alo round 'is 'ead. Way, they were freetened to deeath were shepherds an' med ready to mek a dash for it. "Hold up," says t'hangel, "there's nowt to be frit abaat. I'm not gunna urt thee. I've summat to tell thee. I've cum down to earth to bring thee reight good tidings," an' then 'e tells 'em abaat babby what's been born that neet in Bethli'em. "Let's gu and see 'im," says one o' t'shepherds. An' so away they went, leaving t'sheep to fend for theselves. While all this were goin' on, there were these three Wise Men following yonder big star what sparkled in t'dark sky. After a bit of travellin', they came to a champion palace an' inside were a very nasty piece of work called 'Erod. "We're lookin' for a babby king," t'Wise Men told 'im. "Hast seen 'im?" "Nay," says 'Erod, " 'e's not 'ere, but appen if tha finds this babby king, come back an' tell me, will tha?" He 'ad it in 'is 'ead to kill that babby. "There's only gunna be one king round 'ere," he towld 'imself, "an' that's gunna be me. Mek no mistake abaat that." Soon enough, shepherds an' Wise Men arrived at Bethli'em an' they found Babby Jesus layin' in a manger. "By the heck, 'e's an 'andsome little feller," said t'shepherds. " 'E is that," said t'Wise Men, "an' I'll tell thee what, things are gunna change around here from now on. This little un layin' in t'manger's gunna light up people's lives like that yonder bright star in t'sky." And wi' that, they all knelt dahn before that little babby an' worshipped 'im, for 'e were t'Son of God, t'light o' world."

The boy, who had been staring out of the window while he had related this astonishing story, licked his lips, wrinkled his nose and then looked up at me. "Tha knaas, Mester Phinn," he said thoughtfully, mi granddad says that people sometimes forget t'real meanin' of Christmas. It's nowt to do wi' presents an food an such, he says. It's abaat that little babby in a cowld dark barn wi' nowt but t'bits of cloth what 'e were wrapped up in. Specially at Christmas, we should be thankful for what we've got an' remember them what have nowt. That's what mi granddad says."

"Wise words," I said again.

On that cold, raw December day, when a watery winter sun pierced the high feathery clouds making the snow glow a golden pink, and when the air was so icy it burnt my cheeks and ears, I stood at the gates of the school for a moment. I looked down on the panorama of white, the deep valleys with long grey farmhouses, the meandering river, the omnipresent sheep, the endless limestone walls, and I felt glad to be alive.

ACKNOWLEDGEMENTS AND
SOURCES OF READINGS

My grateful thanks to the people mentioned below for their time, their encouragement, assistance, advice and efforts in helping to complete this Anthology. If I have inadvertently omitted to acknowledge anyone whose material is still in copyright, I hope that you will accept the inclusion of your work as a tribute to you and the pleasure that you have provided for all the readers of this publication.

Texts and Extracts:
Christmas Salutation reproduced from Tasha Tudor's Christmas book, *'Take Joy'* with the permission of the Author and her Publishers - The World Publishing Company, USA; Extract from *'Cider With Rosie'* by Laurie Lee, reproduced with permission from the Publishers, Heinemann of London; extract from *'A Child's Christmas in Wales'* by Dylan Thomas, reproduced with permission from the Trustees for the copyrights of the late Dylan Thomas, through the Publishers, J.M.Dent &Sons Ltd, London; extract *Christmas is Coming* from *'The Country Child'* by Alison Uttley, reproduced with permission from the Publishers, Faber&Faber Ltd; extract *Peace on Earth* by Nina Mansell reproduced from *'A Wartime Christmas Book'*, compiled by Maria and Andrew Hubert and published by Sutton Publishing; extracts *Scrooge's debate with his nephew Fred concerning Christmas* and *The Cratchits' Christmas* from *'A Christmas Carol'*; extract *Mistletoe* from *'The Pickwick Papers'* and *A Dickensian Christmas* from *'Sketches by Boz'* all by Charles Dickens; extract *They Tied a Label on my Coat* by Hilda Hollingsworth from book of the same title, published in 1992 by Virago Press Ltd and used with their permission; extract *A Farmhouse Christmas in London's Blitz* reproduced from *'A Wartime Christmas Book'*, compiled by Maria and Andrew Hubert, published by Sutton Publishing; extract *On This Day* from *'Salute of the Guns'* by Donald Boyd, published by Jonathan Cape, 1930, reproduced with permission of the Publishers and kindly passed on to me by my good friends, Karen and Steve Norris; extract *Prisoner in Germany* from *'Monica - a Heroine of the Danish Resistance'* by Christine Sutherland, reproduced with permission from the Author through Publishers Canongate Press, Scotland; extract *Sojourn in Theresienstadt* from *'A Conspiracy of Decency - The rescue of the Danish Jews during World War II'* by

Emmy E. Werner, reproduced with permission from Publishers Westview Press Oxford; extracts *Snow Fights* and *Carol Singing* from '*Reuben's Corner*' by Spike Mays reproduced with permission from the Publishers, Eyre and Spottiswoode, 1969; extract *Siren Night and Silent Night* by Brian Mellish (MS), reproduced by courtesy of the author; extract *Tea Party* from '*Most Happy Husbandman*' by Ethelind Fearon, Published by Macdonald & Co., 1946; extract *Bring in the Holly* from '*The Scythe in the Apple Tree*' by C. Henry Warren published by Robert Hale Ltd., reproduced by courtesy of the estate of C. Henry Warren; extract *A Country Doctor's Christmas* from '*Country Doctor*' by Geoffrey Barber, reproduced with permission from Publishers Boydell & Brewer, 1974; extract *Christmas in a Village* from '*The Shepherd's Calendar*' by John Clare, reproduced from '*The Christmas Book*' by James Reeves with permission from Publishers Heinemann London, 1968; extract from *Sketch Book* by Washington Irving and extract from *Lark Rise to Candleford* by Flora Thompson, reproduced from '*The Country Diary Christmas Book*' by Sarah Hollis with permission from Publishers Michael Joseph Ltd, through The Penguin Group London; *Christmas Through a Knothole* by Katharine Gibson, *Babouska* by Carolyn Sherwin Bailey and *The Night Before Christmas* by Clement C. Moore taken from '*The Tall Christmas Book*' selected by Dorothy Hall Smith, with permission from Publishers Western Publishing Company Inc. USA; extract *Christmas Underground* from '*The Wind in the Willows*' by Kenneth Grahame, reproduced with permission from Publishers Methuen & Co. Ltd.; extracts from '*A Wayne in a Manger*' and *A Yorkshire Nativity* by Gervase Phinn, reproduced with kind permission from the Author; *Rudolph's Autobiography* by Oliver Pritchett, first published in The Daily Telegraph Newspaper, reproduced with kind permission from the Author; extract *William Joins the Waits* taken from '*Just William at Christmas*' by Richmal Crompton, reproduced with permission from Richmal C Ashbee through Publishers Macmillan Children's Books 1995; poem *My Twelve Days of Christmas*, Author unknown, kindly passed on to me by my good friends Tony and Kathleen Tuckwell; *Call me Blessed* by Jacqueline Wilson, reproduced from '*The Oxford Book of Christmas Stories*' with kind permission from the Author through Publishers Oxford University Press; *The Oxen* by Thomas Hardy from '*The Complete Poems*', Published by Macmillan London Ltd 1976, reproduced with permission from Papermac; *The March of the Three Kings* by Ursula Vaughan Williams from *'Hodie'* by Ralph Vaughan Williams, reproduced by permission of Ursula Vaughan Williams; *Journey of the Magi* from *'The Complete Poems and Plays of T.S.Eliot'* by T.S.Eliot, copyright Valerie Eliot, reproduced with permission of The Book club associates by arrangement with Faber & Faber Ltd.

My very great thanks to the following for making so many things easier for me in the way of detail concerning lay-out, finance, printing and in providing many other useful hints for completing this project in such a professional way;
Joy and Roger Bome, Richard and Jill Vidler, the Caprice Committee Members, Alan Berris and The Printing Place Ltd for their generosity with Sponsorship and the final copy, and most importantly to Ken Rolf for his exquisite illustrations which have added so much to the quality and enjoyment in creating this anthology. I should also like to thank Penny, my wife for all her support and encouragement and last but by no means unrecognised, you the reader, for purchasing a copy of this book and thus contributing to the local Charity Organisations being supported by Caprice.

Thank you one and all!

Jon Vaughan